Science and Tech Sense

Andrew E. Bennett

NAN'UN-DO

Science and Tech Sense

Copyright © 2019
by Andrew E. Bennett

All Rights Reserved
No part of this book may be reproduced in any form
without written permission from the authors and Nan'un-do Co.,Ltd.

Written and designed by Andrew E. Bennett
Technical Focus Illustrations: Irene Fu

このテキストの音声を無料で視聴（ストリーミング）・ダウンロードできます。自習用音声としてご活用ください。
以下のサイトにアクセスしてテキスト番号で検索してください。

https://nanun-do.com　テキスト番号 [511978]

※ 無線 LAN（WiFi）に接続してのご利用を推奨いたします。
※ 音声ダウンロードは Zip ファイルでの提供になります。
　お使いの機器によっては別途ソフトウェア（アプリケーション）の導入が必要となります。

※ Science and Tech Sense 音声ダウンロードページは
以下の QR コードからもご利用になれます。

Introduction

In *Science and Tech Sense*, units are organized around a 400-word article on a topic, trend, or breakthrough in a scientific field. A range of fields are covered, including medicine, physics, astronomy, biology, engineering, and more. The articles, as well as the book's exercises, are set at an intermediate level. The reading passages are designed to be understandable and interesting to all students, regardless of their major. What's more, vocabulary and grammar levels are carefully maintained to maximize comprehension while gradually building language abilities.

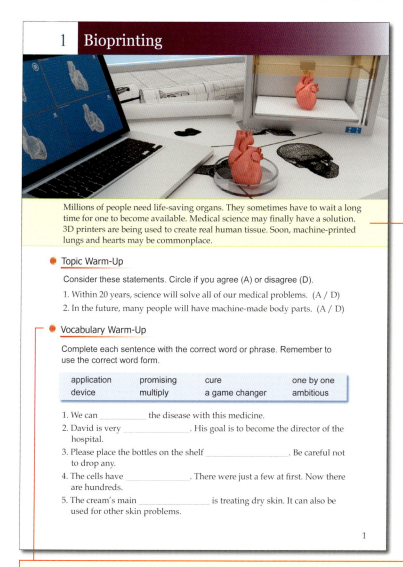

Units open with a warm-up page. First there is a short introductory paragraph. This passage is designed to get students thinking about the topic so they can scaffold their own prior knowledge. Next is a warm-up exercise containing two statements which students can agree or disagree with. These statements, which are related to the unit's topic, can also be discussed in pairs, small groups, or together as a class. Finally on the first page, there is a vocabulary warm-up exercise checking students' knowledge of the unit's target vocabulary items.

There are eight target vocabulary items per unit. They were chosen for their frequency of use and suitability when talking or reading about the topic. These items may be single words or phrases such as common expressions, phrasal verbs, and colloquialisms.

● Reading Passage Track 2

From making art to crafting eye glasses, 3D printers are reshaping our world. One of their most **promising** uses is in medicine. As the name suggests, "bioprinting" uses living cells to print human tissue. Its **applications** include testing drugs and treating injuries. Years from now,
5 bioprinting may even **cure** people waiting for new hearts, livers, and other organs.

On a mechanical level, a bioprinter combines several technologies. It starts with a computer that supplies a model of the object being printed. As the bioprinter moves around, it acts like an inkjet printer, delivering
10 cell droplets **one by one**. Since it is a 3D printer, the **device** can move up, down, and in other directions. Tissues slowly grow as they are printed one layer at a time.

The creation of a bioprinter's cell droplets, called "bioink," is fascinating. First, living
15 cells are cultured in a laboratory, allowing them to **multiply**. Thousands of cells are gathered into a single droplet of bioink. During the printing process, one print head delivers the bioink. Another delivers
20 "biopaper," a gel or other material that supports the growing tissue.

The first bioprinter was made in 2008 by Professor Makoto Nakamura. He used it to create "biotubing" that worked like a blood vessel. The following year, California-based Organovo built its NovoGen MMX Bioprinter. By 2014, the company was printing human liver tissue for
25 use in drug testing. That's one of the technology's main applications. By working with material that acts like human tissue, drug companies can reduce animal testing. They can also speed up drug development schedules.

A more **ambitious** goal for the technology is the creation of body parts
30 such as bones and organs. That's a challenging task. Printing something that behaves like a kidney is one thing. Making the organ stable and long lasting is another. But progress is being made. For example, Cornell University researchers are working on printing heart valves. And scientists at Harvard University have used silicon molds to make thicker,
35 longer-lasting tissue.

Perhaps the greatest hope for bioprinting is in personalized medicine. One day, a patient's own cells may be used to create bioink to print a custom-made organ. The process would make it easier for his or her body to accept the replacement. Such an advance would be **a game**
40 **changer**, saving millions of lives. With many researchers hard at work, bioprinting could soon become a key medical tool. It may even make organ waitlists a thing of the past.

Glossary
tissue – group of cells that form organs and other body parts; droplet – small drop; fascinating – very interesting; cultured – grown; speed up – make faster; task – job; heart valve – part of the heart that opens and closes to let blood through; personalized – made for a specific person; a thing of the past – something that doesn't exist anymore

● Comprehension Check

Choose the best answer to each question.
Main Idea
1. What is the main idea?
   (A) Many patients must wait a long time for organ transplants.
   (B) Drug companies are doing most of the research into bioprinting.
   (C) Bioprinters make human tissue for important medical uses.
   (D) Besides bioprinting, 3D printers are used for a variety of tasks.
Detail
2. How is a bioprinter like a 3D printer?
   (A) It can move in many directions.   (B) It only prints flat objects.
   (C) It prints things using black ink.   (D) It sends images to a computer.
Analysis
3. What does the article suggest about bioprinting organs?
   (A) We can already print every kind of organ for transplant use.
   (B) Patients' bodies will reject organs that are bioprinted.
   (C) Bioprinting organs is easier than bioprinting bones.
   (D) It is still hard to print organs that will last a long time.

Circle if each statement is true (T) or false (F).

1. A droplet of bioink contains thousands of living cells. (T / F)
2. Organovo created the NovoGen MMX Bioprinter in 2008. (T / F)

The fourth page of each unit starts with a pair of vocabulary exercises. Between them, all eight of the unit's target vocabulary items are tested. The first exercise is a set of five multiple choice cloze sentences. For the second exercise, students choose the word or phrase that means the same as the underlined part.

- **Vocabulary Check**

    A. Choose the best word or phrase to complete each sentence.
    1. Over the years, the number of fish in the lake has _____.
       (A) combined   (B) printed   (C) multiplied   (D) treated
    2. _____, the doctors entered the room. They were about to begin a difficult operation.
       (A) One by one   (B) Years from now   (C) Long lasting   (D) A thing of the past
    3. The new drug is a(n) _____. It works for 90% of the patients that take it.
       (A) organ waitlist   (B) mechanical level
       (C) printing process   (D) game changer
    4. Linda is not very _____. She is happy cleaning the office building, and she doesn't want a better job there.
       (A) single   (B) ambitious   (C) delivered   (D) stable
    5. There's a red light on the _____. It tells you when the machine is turned on.
       (A) device   (B) technology   (C) tissue   (D) layer

    B. Choose the word or phrase that means the same as the underlined part.
    1. The research hospital's technique for treating cancer patients is promising.
       (A) expensive   (B) hopeful   (C) unknown   (D) different
    2. My dad says the best way to cure a cold is to get plenty of rest.
       (A) make better   (B) spread around   (C) look into   (D) forget about
    3. Common medicines like aspirin have many applications.
       (A) prices   (B) sizes   (C) clinics   (D) uses

- **Grammar Building - Adjective Clauses**

    Choose the correct word to complete each sentence.

    Ex: A bioprinter is a machine (that / who) prints human tissue.
    Ans: A bioprinter is a machine *that* prints human tissue.

    1. Professor Nakamura is a scientist (who / where) has made important findings.
    2. This is the laboratory (that / where) the cells are cultured.
    3. The hospital has dozens of patients (where / who) are waiting for new organs.
    4. Harvard researchers use silicon molds (that / who) help tissue last longer.
    5. Organovo is doing work (where / which) is famous in the bioprinting field.

Next, there is a grammar exercise. It is based on a language structure found in the reading passage. First, a sample item and its answer are given. Then, five items check students' understanding of the structure.

The fifth page starts with an exercise that combines the unit's target grammar structure and target vocabulary items. Students arrange a series of words and phrases into the correct sentence order. The answers should be written on the lines provided.

Next is a unique Technical Focus section. It starts with an illustration or diagram of something related to the unit. For example, Unit 1 contains a drawing of a 3D printer. Unit 3 shows a spacecraft's approach and departure from an asteroid. In books, journals, and websites, science and technology articles frequently contain visual aids. The drawings and annotations in *Science and Tech Sense* are designed to be understandable to all students, regardless of their field of specialty. The goal is to give students more exposure to visual aids, enriching their study of the topic while expanding their English skill set.

● Grammar + Vocabulary

Put the words in the correct sentence order.

1. (who wants to / researcher / cure cancer / an ambitious / He is).
   _____

2. (air pressure / a device / measures / A barometer / which / is).
   _____

● Technical Focus

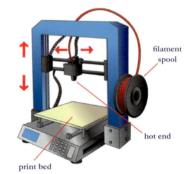

A. Look at the illustration of a 3D printer. Then, circle if each statement is true (T) or false (F).

1. A wire is wound around the filament spool. (T / F)
2. The print bed is at the very top of the machine. (T / F)
3. Some parts of the printer move up and down or left and right. (T / F)

B. Fill in the blanks with the correct word(s) from the box.

| positions | which | finish |
| one of | with | challenges |

For a 3D bioprinter, the accurate positioning of the print heads is very important. It's 1)_____ the key engineering 2)_____ of designing a bioprinter. To create the NovoGen MMX Bioprinter, Organovo partnered 3)_____ Invetech. It only took the company, 4)_____ is in the same city as Organovo, nine months to 5)_____ the task. Invetech did an amazing job. A computer-controlled laser 6)_____ the print heads with great accuracy.

Accompanying each illustration or diagram are three true or false statements. They are followed by a cloze paragraph which provides more details about the item under focus. A box containing six words or phrases is given. The paragraph beneath the box has six blanks, and each item from the box should be used only once.

The final page of each unit starts with a word parts exercise. It presents three word parts which are found in the reading passage. There is one prefix, one root, and one suffix. The meaning for each of them is given. Also, three example words are provided. The first example is the word from the reading passage that the prefix, root, or suffix is based on.

● Word Parts

Study the word parts in the chart. Then, read the following pairs of sentences. Circle if the second sentence is true (T) or false (F).

Word Part	Meaning	Examples
re-	again	reshape, revise, reconsider
-bio-	life	bioprinting, symbiotic, bionic
-ory	related to a place	laboratory, observatory, conservatory

1. The lab technicians are redoing the test to verify the results.
   It's their first time trying the test. (T / F)

2. The biographer spent years learning about Marie Curie.
   The biographer researched Curie's life. (T / F)

3. We can check the contents of the book depository online.
   The depository is the person who organizes the books. (T / F)

4. Earth's biosphere goes from deep underground to high above the planet.
   Life is found below, on, and above the planet. (T / F)

5. My supervisor said we should redesign the neck brace.
   The neck brace needs to be designed one more time. (T / F)

Next is an exercise containing three items that check students' understanding of the word parts. After reading the first statement, students should read the second one and circle if it is true or false.

● Discussion

Discuss these questions with your classmates.

1. In your opinion, what are the most promising uses of bioprinters?
2. What are some medical challenges that could soon be solved by science?

Finally, there is a discussion exercise with two questions about the topic. This is an opportunity for students to use the language tools (such as the target vocabulary items) learned in the unit. It's also a chance for students to provide their own perspectives and opinions.

As one possible classroom activity, if the discussion exercise is done in pairs or in small groups, one student can take notes, and after a few minutes, the pairs or groups can share their results with the whole class. Or the class might prefer to answer the questions together. The exercise can even be turned into a short writing assignment, with students asked to use some of the unit's target vocabulary items and/or the target grammar structure while answering one of the questions.

Thank you very much for choosing *Science and Tech Sense*. I hope it broadens your students' perspectives while helping make your classes more engaging and successful!

Andrew E. Bennett

Contents

Introduction...iv

1. Bioprinting..1
2. Driverless Cars...7
3. Space Mining..13
4. Big Data...19
5. Rethinking Animal Intelligence...25
6. Getting Chipped...31
7. New Advances in Architecture... 37
8. Making Science Popular: The Brilliance of Carl Sagan.....43
9. Extreme Weather and Climate Change............................49
10. Virtual Reality in Medicine..55
11. Should we fear intelligent machines?.......................... 61
12. Megacities... 67
13. De-Extinction.. 73
14. Muon Imaging: Using Physics to See the Unseen.......... 79
15. Our Clean Future..85

1 Bioprinting

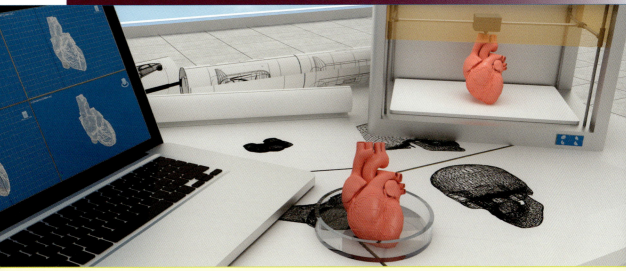

 Track 2

Millions of people need life-saving organs. They sometimes have to wait a long time for one to become available. Medical science may finally have a solution. 3D printers are being used to create real human tissue. Soon, machine-printed lungs and hearts may be commonplace.

● Topic Warm-Up

Consider these statements. Circle if you agree (A) or disagree (D).

1. Within 20 years, science will solve all of our medical problems. (A / D)
2. In the future, many people will have machine-made body parts. (A / D)

● Vocabulary Warm-Up

Complete each sentence with the correct word or phrase. Remember to use the correct word form.

| application | promising | cure | one by one |
| device | multiply | a game changer | ambitious |

1. We can _____ the disease with this medicine.
2. David is very _____. His goal is to become the director of the hospital.
3. Please place the bottles on the shelf _____. Be careful not to drop any.
4. The cells have _____. There were just a few at first. Now there are hundreds.
5. The cream's main _____ is treating dry skin. It can also be used for other skin problems.

1

Reading Passage

From making art to crafting eye glasses, 3D printers are reshaping our world. One of their most **promising** uses is in medicine. As the name suggests, "bioprinting" uses living cells to print human tissue. Its **applications** include testing drugs and treating injuries. Years from now, bioprinting may even **cure** people waiting for new hearts, livers, and other organs.

On a mechanical level, a bioprinter combines several technologies. It starts with a computer that supplies a model of the object being printed. As the bioprinter moves around, it acts like an inkjet printer, delivering cell droplets **one by one**. Since it is a 3D printer, the **device** can move up, down, and in other directions. Tissues slowly grow as they are printed one layer at a time.

The creation of a bioprinter's cell droplets, called "bioink," is fascinating. First, living cells are cultured in a laboratory, allowing them to **multiply**. Thousands of cells are gathered into a single droplet of bioink. During the printing process, one print head delivers the bioink. Another delivers "biopaper," a gel or other material that supports the growing tissue.

The first bioprinter was made in 2008 by Professor Makoto Nakamura. He used it to create "biotubing" that worked like a blood vessel. The following year, California-based Organovo built its NovoGen MMX Bioprinter. By 2014, the company was printing human liver tissue for use in drug testing. That's one of the technology's main applications. By working with material that acts like human tissue, drug companies can reduce animal testing. They can also speed up drug development schedules.

A more **ambitious** goal for the technology is the creation of body parts such as bones and organs. That's a challenging task. Printing something that behaves like a kidney is one thing. Making the organ stable and long lasting is another. But progress is being made. For example, Cornell University researchers are working on printing heart valves. And scientists at Harvard University have used silicon molds to make thicker, longer-lasting tissue.

Perhaps the greatest hope for bioprinting is in personalized medicine. One day, a patient's own cells may be used to create bioink to print a custom-made organ. The process would make it easier for his or her body to accept the replacement. Such an advance would be **a game changer**, saving millions of lives. With many researchers hard at work, bioprinting could soon become a key medical tool. It may even make organ waitlists a thing of the past.

> **Glossary**
> tissue – group of cells that form organs and other body parts; droplet – small drop; fascinating – very interesting; cultured – grown; speed up – make faster; task – job; heart valve – part of the heart that opens and closes to let blood through; personalized – made for a specific person; a thing of the past – something that doesn't exist anymore

Comprehension Check

Choose the best answer to each question.

Main Idea
1. What is the main idea?
   (A) Many patients must wait a long time for organ transplants.
   (B) Drug companies are doing most of the research into bioprinting.
   (C) Bioprinters make human tissue for important medical uses.
   (D) Besides bioprinting, 3D printers are used for a variety of tasks.

Detail
2. How is a bioprinter like a 3D printer?
   (A) It can move in many directions.   (B) It only prints flat objects.
   (C) It prints things using black ink.   (D) It sends images to a computer.

Analysis
3. What does the article suggest about bioprinting organs?
   (A) We can already print every kind of organ for transplant use.
   (B) Patients' bodies will reject organs that are bioprinted.
   (C) Bioprinting organs is easier than bioprinting bones.
   (D) It is still hard to print organs that will last a long time.

Circle if each statement is true (T) or false (F).

1. A droplet of bioink contains thousands of living cells. (T / F)

2. Organovo created the NovoGen MMX Bioprinter in 2008. (T / F)

● Vocabulary Check

A. Choose the best word or phrase to complete each sentence.
1. Over the years, the number of fish in the lake has _____.
   (A) combined   (B) printed   (C) multiplied   (D) treated
2. _____, the doctors entered the room. They were about to begin a difficult operation.
   (A) One by one   (B) Years from now   (C) Long lasting   (D) A thing of the past
3. The new drug is a(n) _____. It works for 90% of the patients that take it.
   (A) organ waitlist   (B) mechanical level
   (C) printing process   (D) game changer
4. Linda is not very _____. She is happy cleaning the office building, and she doesn't want a better job there.
   (A) single   (B) ambitious   (C) delivered   (D) stable
5. There's a red light on the _____. It tells you when the machine is turned on.
   (A) device   (B) technology   (C) tissue   (D) layer

B. Choose the word or phrase that means the same as the underlined part.
1. The research hospital's technique for treating cancer patients is <u>promising</u>.
   (A) expensive   (B) hopeful   (C) unknown   (D) different
2. My dad says the best way to <u>cure</u> a cold is to get plenty of rest.
   (A) make better (B) spread around (C) look into   (D) forget about
3. Common medicines like aspirin have many <u>applications</u>.
   (A) prices   (B) sizes   (C) clinics   (D) uses

● Grammar Building - Adjective Clauses

Choose the correct word to complete each sentence.

Ex: A bioprinter is a machine (that / who) prints human tissue.
Ans: A bioprinter is a machine *that* prints human tissue.

1. Professor Nakamura is a scientist (who / where) has made important findings.
2. This is the laboratory (that / where) the cells are cultured.
3. The hospital has dozens of patients (where / who) are waiting for new organs.
4. Harvard researchers use silicon molds (that / who) help tissue last longer.
5. Organovo is doing work (where / which) is famous in the bioprinting field.

Grammar + Vocabulary

Put the words in the correct sentence order.

1. (who wants to / researcher / cure cancer / an ambitious / He is).

   _____

2. (air pressure / a device / measures / A barometer / which / is).

   _____

Technical Focus

A. Look at the illustration of a 3D printer. Then, circle if each statement is true (T) or false (F).

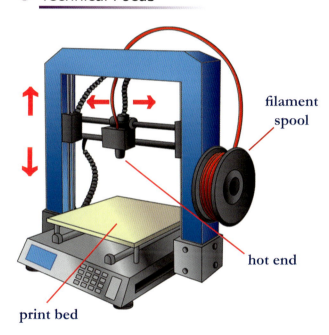

1. A wire is wound around the filament spool. (T / F)
2. The print bed is at the very top of the machine. (T / F)
3. Some parts of the printer move up and down or left and right. (T / F)

B. Fill in the blanks with the correct word(s) from the box.

positions	which	finish
one of	with	challenges

For a 3D bioprinter, the accurate positioning of the print heads is very important. It's 1)_____ the key engineering 2)_____ of designing a bioprinter. To create the NovoGen MMX Bioprinter, Organovo partnered 3)_____ Invetech. It only took the company, 4)_____ is in the same city as Organovo, nine months to 5)_____ the task. Invetech did an amazing job. A computer-controlled laser 6)_____ the print heads with great accuracy.

Word Parts

Study the word parts in the chart. Then, read the following pairs of sentences. Circle if the second sentence is true (T) or false (F).

Word Part	Meaning	Examples
re-	again	reshape, revise, reconsider
-bio-	life	bioprinting, symbiotic, bionic
-ory	related to a place	laboratory, observatory, conservatory

1. The lab technicians are redoing the test to verify the results.
   It's their first time trying the test. (T / F)

2. The biographer spent years learning about Marie Curie.
   The biographer researched Curie's life. (T / F)

3. We can check the contents of the book depository online.
   The depository is the person who organizes the books. (T / F)

4. Earth's biosphere goes from deep underground to high above the planet.
   Life is found below, on, and above the planet. (T / F)

5. My supervisor said we should redesign the neck brace.
   The neck brace needs to be designed one more time. (T / F)

Discussion

Discuss these questions with your classmates.

1. In your opinion, what are the most promising uses of bioprinters?

2. What are some medical challenges that could soon be solved by science?

2 Driverless Cars

 Track 4   Cars are a central feature of modern life. However, along with them come accidents, air pollution, and other problems. The world's leading car and technology companies are working on cars that drive themselves. These 21st century vehicles will make roads cleaner and safer.

● Topic Warm-Up

Consider these statements. Circle if you agree (A) or disagree (D).

1. In the future, I want to own a car. (A / D)
2. Cars that are completely controlled by computers will be safe. (A / D)

● Vocabulary Warm-Up

Complete each sentence with the correct word or phrase. Remember to use the correct word form.

category	real estate	potential	rate
efficient	drawback	analyze	overhaul

1. Unfortunately, the building project will be expensive. That's its biggest _____.
2. We need to _____ this data. Our job is to understand why traffic is bad downtown.
3. It's a really _____ machine. It scans 1,000 pages in five minutes.
4. The city is growing at a fast _____. Since 1990, it has doubled in size.
5. Cars in the "all-electric" _____ are clean, and they create very little pollution.

7

Reading Passage Track 5

Some inventions make our lives easier. Others make us safer. Driverless cars have the **potential** to do both. It's a cutting-edge field with companies racing to **overhaul** one of the world's biggest industries. If everything goes as planned, it may soon be common to sit back and relax as robotic cars drive us around.

Self-driving cars fall into two main **categories**. First, there are "autonomous" cars. They can be controlled by a person, a computer, or a combination of the two. General Motors already has a fleet of these cars in San Francisco. The second, more advanced type of driverless car is entirely controlled by computers and may not even have a steering wheel. Nissan, Tesla, Volvo, and other car companies are involved in this field. So are technology and service firms like Apple, Uber, and Intel.

Both varieties are powered by AI (artificial intelligence) brains which start by gathering information about road conditions. The cars' tools include cameras, sensors, GPS, and lidar (a combination of laser and radar). Details are compiled about other vehicles, bikes, pedestrians, and more, creating a virtual image of the surroundings. After the AI **analyzes** the information, it tells the car to stop, go, turn, and so on.

There are pros and cons to these amazing vehicles. On the plus side, they are considered very safe. Currently, 90% of accidents are caused by driver error. Self-driving cars could greatly reduce the accident **rate**. Plus, since these automobiles are highly **efficient**, air pollution and road congestion will decrease. There's also the matter of parking lots, which use up to 30% of the **real estate** in some cities. Once a passenger exits a driverless car, it can simply continue on its way without parking. That means the asphalt covering parking lots can be replaced with beautiful green grass.

Yet there are **drawbacks**. While trucking companies will save billions of dollars by switching to driverless fleets, millions of drivers will lose their jobs. There are also safety concerns over hackers taking control of robotic vehicles. Furthermore, a malfunction in the electronics or AI could have terrible consequences.

As we transition to driverless cars, cities will need to adjust. At first, they'll likely have to build special road lanes. Traffic lights will also need upgrading so they can communicate with smart vehicles. Such investments should be worth it. According to research by Strategic Analytics, the industry shift will lead to many business opportunities, adding seven trillion dollars to the global economy. That incredible payout may be the main fuel moving us towards a self-driven future.

> **Glossary**
> cutting-edge – highly advanced; autonomous – self-directed and self-controlled; fleet – group of automobiles; GPS – Global Positioning System; compiled – put together; pedestrian – person walking outside; vehicle – car, truck, or other automobile; road congestion – situation in which roads are crowded; asphalt – black material that covers roads; billion – 1,000,000,000; hacker – person who breaks into computer systems; malfunction – machine error; consequence – result; transition – shift; trillion – 1,000,000,000,000

Comprehension Check

Choose the best answer to each question.

Main Idea
1. What is the main idea?
    (A) General Motors is the world's leading producer of driverless vehicles.
    (B) Both automobile and technology companies spend heavily on research.
    (C) In modern times, every major invention has pros and cons to consider.
    (D) Though not perfect, driverless cars are safe and good for the economy.

Detail
2. Which of these is NOT considered a problem with driverless cars?
    (A) The accident rate will go up.
    (B) Hackers could break into control systems.
    (C) Many truck drivers will be fired.
    (D) An error with the AI might be very serious.

Analysis
3. What does the article suggest about parking lots?
    (A) Once driverless cars are common, we will need fewer parking lots.
    (B) Special lots will be built for driverless cars.
    (C) Real estate developers will turn parking lots into new office buildings.
    (D) In the future, they will be 30% smaller.

Circle if each statement is true (T) or false (F).

1. Autonomous cars don't need steering wheels since they are always controlled by computers. (T / F)

2. Using "lidar" is one way a driverless car learns about road conditions. (T / F)

● Vocabulary Check

A. Choose the best word or phrase to complete each sentence.
1. This is some of Shanghai's best _____. The land is especially valuable.
   (A) road congestion (B) global economy (C) real estate (D) air pollution
2. It takes our workers weeks to do simple repairs. To save time and money, let's find a more _____ method.
   (A) efficient   (B) terrible   (C) entire   (D) common
3. Cars on this street need to slow down. The accident _____ is far too high.
   (A) rate   (B) fleet   (C) tool   (D) lot
4. While riding in driverless cars, people can shop online. The _____ for companies to make money this way is significant.
   (A) combination (B) pedestrian (C) potential (D) condition
5. Our team has _____ the vehicle. Making it 15% lighter would be a good way to reduce its fuel needs.
   (A) involved   (B) caused   (C) reduced   (D) analyzed

B. Choose the word that means the same as the underlined part.
1. The road system needs to be overhauled to prepare the city for driverless cars.
   (A) overseen   (B) supported   (C) studied   (D) revised
2. GPS systems don't work well in some areas. It's a drawback of driverless cars.
   (A) blueprint   (B) problem   (C) suggestion (D) engineer
3. Young people fall into the category of city residents who love ride sharing services.
   (A) type   (B) driver   (C) fee   (D) situation

● Grammar Building - Present Participle vs. Past Participle

Circle the correct word to complete each sentence.

Ex: Temperature levels are (maintaining / maintained) by a central cooling system.
Ans: Temperature levels are *maintained* by a central cooling system.

1. AI is (finding / found) in everything from video games to call centers.
2. Google is (spending / spent) millions of dollars developing driverless cars.
3. Have you (compiling / compiled) the data for the fuel efficiency report?
4. What is (considering / considered) the best electric car on the market?
5. (Switching / Switched) to driverless cars will take everyone time to get used to.

Grammar + Vocabulary

Put the words in the correct sentence order.

1. (the information / are / the report / analyzing / We / from).

___

2. (take / highways may / Overhauling / all the / years).

___

Technical Focus

A. Look at the illustration of a Waymo driverless car. Then, circle if each statement is true (T) or false (F).

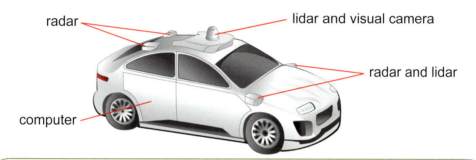

1. A visual camera system is on top of the car. (T / F)
2. The car has multiple lidar and radar systems. (T / F)
3. At the front and back ends of the car, there are computers which analyze the sensor information. (T / F)

B. Fill in each blank with the correct word from the box.

as	around	each
owned	conditions	safe

Waymo, which is 1)_____ by Google, builds the tech giant's driverless cars. 2)_____ car has advanced sensors that collect information. A camera sees all 3)_____ the vehicle, creating a 360-degree view of the road. Lidar identifies objects as far 4)_____ 180 meters away. Even in bad weather, built-in radar provides a picture of road 5)_____. Super-fast software puts all the information together for a 6)_____ driving experience.

● Word Parts

Study the word parts in the chart. Then, read the following pairs of sentences. Circle if the second sentence is true (T) or false (F).

Word Part	Meaning	Examples
com	with / together	compile, combine, communicate
-mob-	related to movement	automobile, mobility, immobile
-less	without	driverless, spotless, nameless

1. Table salt is a compound made of sodium and chloride.
   Sodium and chloride come together to make table salt. (T / F)

2. Chinese painter Huang Guofu may be armless, but he still makes beautiful artwork.
   Huang Guofu sometimes paints with his feet and sometimes with his hands. (T / F)

3. In winter, my neighbors use snowmobiles for transportation.
   Snowmobiles help them move around in winter. (T / F)

4. After the storm, parts of Manila were powerless for two days.
   Some Manila residents didn't have power for 48 hours. (T / F)

5. The two tech giants will combine forces to develop a driverless car.
   Each company is planning to work alone to produce a vehicle. (T / F)

● Discussion

Discuss these questions with your classmates.

1. More and more jobs are being done by machines and computers. In your opinion, is that a good thing, a bad thing, or both? Why?

2. Cities of the future may need fewer parking lots. How should cities reuse the land?

3 Space Mining

Track 6

Our spacecraft have already flown far beyond the Earth. Soon, national space programs and private companies may begin to actively use metals and other resources found in space. Such mining operations could greatly affect the future of space exploration.

Topic Warm-Up

Consider these statements. Circle if you agree (A) or disagree (D).

1. Private companies are doing important work in space exploration. (A / D)
2. In the future, living and working in space will be common. (A / D)

Vocabulary Warm-Up

Complete each sentence with the correct word or phrase. Remember to use the correct word form.

| launch | candidate | explore | in motion |
| on the cusp of | valuable | fuel | complicated |

1. Traveling to another planet takes a huge amount of _____ and other resources.
2. Our team is _____ finishing the engine design. We just need a little more time.
3. Large, flat places make good _____ for new airports.
4. Spacecraft are so _____ that it takes teams of experts years to build them.
5. When a rocket _____, the surrounding area becomes extremely hot.

Reading Passage Track 7

Space is vast and full of mysteries. Although we are slowly unlocking its secrets, **launching** ships and supplies from our planet remains expensive. Space mining may be the solution. Water, metals, and other important resources exist in space in abundance. We are rapidly developing the
5   technology to use these materials to help us **explore** the cosmos.

The moon and Mars are two **candidates** for space mining. We know a great deal about the moon, and it has deposits of ice and Helium-3, a rare **fuel** source. Companies like Japan's ispace have plans to send rovers there. Mars is farther away, but it has metal deposits on its surface. They
10 could be used as building materials by future colonists.

Asteroids are receiving the most attention for space mining. The more than 16,000 "near-Earth" examples are divided into three types. C-type asteroids are the most common. They are rich in
15 carbon, phosphorous, and water. Besides being a drinking source, water can be used for radiation shielding and fuel. Deep Space Industries and Planetary Resources are two companies with plans **in motion** to explore such asteroids.

20 Next, there are S-type asteroids. They have large deposits of iron and nickel as well as small amounts of gold and platinum. In comparison, the third variety of asteroid, M-type, contains 10 times more precious metals. These asteroids are rare and incredibly **valuable**. Within a few decades, we may start digging up their treasure and sending it back to Earth.

25 Mining an asteroid is **complicated**, and we are still developing some of the necessary technology. The first step is identifying suitable candidates by using telescopes. The next stage will be sending small unmanned spacecraft to asteroids for closer analysis. Next, robotic landing craft will extract raw materials from the best choices.

30 The final stages can be carried out by bringing the raw materials back to Earth orbit. There, space-based robotic equipment will separate and process everything. AI-controlled tools and 3D printers might one day build huge ships and structures this way. Another idea is to perform these final steps in deep space, making asteroids "stepping stones" for further
35 space travel.

Thanks to national space agencies like JAXA, NASA, and the ESA, we've already learned a lot about space travel, the moon, Mars, and asteroids. Companies are putting these lessons to work while adding their own innovations. We are **on the cusp of** amazing new discoveries, not to mention incredible wealth creation. Space mining may play a central role in these efforts.

> **Glossary**
> vast – large and wide; abundance – large amount; cosmos – universe; rover – car that explores a surface in space; colonist – one of the first people to move somewhere; asteroid – rocky, space-based object that orbits the sun; shielding – protective cover; precious – valuable / rare; suitable – right for the job; unmanned – without people; extract – remove; Earth orbit – the band of space in which objects circle the Earth; stepping stone – a place or event that helps you reach a goal; JAXA – Japan's space agency; NASA – the USA's space agency; ESA – Europe's space agency; innovation – new idea or invention; not to mention – as well as

Comprehension Check

Choose the best answer to each question.

Main Idea
1. What is the main idea?
   (A) Space mining is expensive because of the high cost of rocket fuel.
   (B) Mining objects in space could advance space travel while making companies rich.
   (C) Deep Space Industries and Planetary Resources have big plans in motion.
   (D) In space, finding new materials for radiation shielding is a very important task.

Detail
2. According to the article, what could be mined on the moon?
   (A) Rovers   (B) Platinum   (C) Carbon   (D) Helium-3

Analysis
3. What does the article suggest about asteroid mining?
   (A) It takes longer to find suitable asteroids than to extract their metals.
   (B) Deep-space metal processing is easier than near-Earth processing.
   (C) C-type asteroids have more phosphorous than water or carbon.
   (D) Asteroid mining and material processing can all be done by robots.

Circle if each statement is true (T) or false (F).

1. Although Mars is far away, its metal deposits could be useful. (T / F)
2. S-type asteroids have more precious metals than M-type asteroids. (T / F)

Vocabulary Check

A. Choose the best word to complete each sentence.

1. The Saturn V rocket used 3.5 million liters of _____ on its moon mission.
   (A) space   (B) fuel   (C) orbit   (D) Mars
2. The top three _____ for the job will meet with us this week.
   (A) candidates   (B) mysteries   (C) asteroids   (D) missions
3. Precious metals like silver are used to make electronics. They are so _____ that they must be kept in a safe place.
   (A) valuable   (B) unmanned   (C) robotic   (D) national
4. If the weather is good, the spacecraft will _____ at 9:45 AM.
   (A) dig   (B) exist   (C) launch   (D) serve
5. The first people to _____ Mars may not be able to return to Earth.
   (A) extract   (B) unlock   (C) contain   (D) explore

B. Choose the word or phrase that means the same as the underlined part.

1. Our plan to build a five-meter telescope is already in motion.
   (A) recording   (B) changing   (C) happening   (D) supporting
2. The engineering group is on the cusp of figuring out the problem.
   (A) very close to   (B) ordering someone to
   (C) finding reasons for   (D) very excited about
3. The computer is so powerful that it can quickly solve complicated math problems.
   (A) previous   (B) difficult   (C) popular   (D) common

Grammar Building - Adjectives vs. Adverbs

Circle the correct word to complete each sentence.

Ex: An astronaut's suit is an (extreme / extremely) important piece of equipment.
Ans: An astronaut's suit is an *extremely* important piece of equipment.

1. For long-distance space travel, finding a (suitable / suitably) fuel source is a must.
2. In the 1960s, the USA and USSR competed on a (national / nationally) level to be the first to reach the moon.
3. Companies like SpaceX have (successful / successfully) sent supplies to the International Space Station.
4. (Rare / Rarely) metals such as gold are easily found on M-type asteroids.
5. Most manned space missions have been completed (safe / safely).

- ## Grammar + Vocabulary

    Put the words in the correct sentence order.

    1. (on the cusp of / Amazingly, / to Mars / we are / sending people).

    _____

    2. (coding job / smart and hard working / for the / is / Every candidate).

    _____

- ## Technical Focus

    A. Look at the illustration of the OSIRIS-REx spacecraft and Bennu asteroid. Then, circle if each statement is true (T) or false (F).

    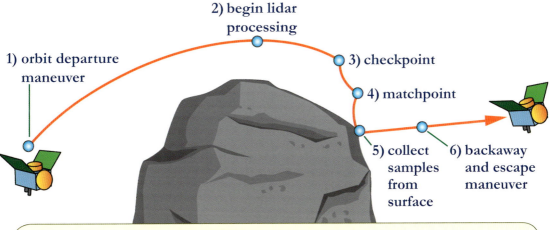

    1. The escape maneuver will happen last. (T / F)
    2. Sample collecting will be the fifth step. (T / F)
    3. OSIRIS-REx will be closest to Bennu during the checkpoint step. (T / F)

    B. Fill in the blanks with the correct word(s) from the box.

surface	its	successfully
back to	exploring	will

    National space agencies have done important work 1)_____ asteroids. In 2000, JAXA 2)_____ carried out the Hayabusa mission. A spacecraft was sent to an asteroid, and material was extracted from the 3)_____ and returned to Earth. In 2016, NASA launched the OSIRIS-REx spacecraft. 4)_____ mission includes flying to the Bennu asteroid and studying it for two years. Then it 5)_____ extract material from the asteroid and fly 6)_____ Earth.

Word Parts

Study the word parts in the chart. Then, read the following pairs of sentences. Circle if the second sentence is true (T) or false (F).

Word Part	Meaning	Examples
un-	not / reverse	unlock, unfair, unevenly
-pos-	place / set	deposit, position, post
-ist	person who does something	colonist, geologist, tourist

1. Midori is studying to be a professional pianist.
   She is a student of the piano. (T / F)

2. The two large viewing windows are on opposite sides of the ship.
   The windows are side by side. (T / F)

3. Due to a dirty filter, oxygen levels were uneven.
   The amount of oxygen stayed the same. (T / F)

4. The equipment repository is in Building C.
   Building C is the place where the equipment is stored. (T / F)

5. We can use this tool to unbend the pipe.
   With the tool, we'll make the pipe straight again. (T / F)

Discussion

Discuss these questions with your classmates.

1. How do you feel about private companies mining objects in space? Should they be allowed to make money from asteroids, the moon, etc.?

2. Future mining jobs may require people to work in space. Would a job like that interest you? Why or why not?

4 Big Data

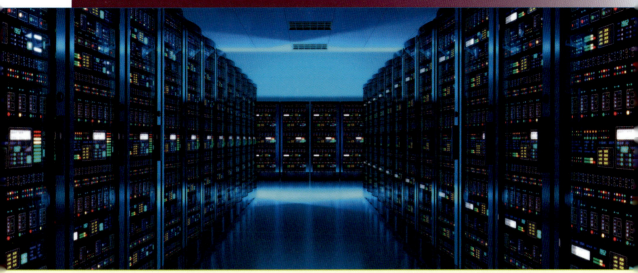

Track 8

To make smart decisions, we need to understand both the past and the present. Big data is very helpful in this process. Using it, businesses and governments analyze information in search of patterns. Then, they can make better plans for the future.

Topic Warm-Up

Consider these statements. Circle if you agree (A) or disagree (D).

1. Online and offline, businesses often ask for my name, address, and birth date. (A / D)
2. I make better decisions when I have more information about something. (A / D)

Vocabulary Warm-Up

Complete each sentence with the correct word or phrase. Remember to use the correct word form.

| relationship | eager | accuracy | call into question |
| impressive | generate | predict | break down |

1. Before big holidays, stores try to _____ which products will be popular. That way, they can prepare enough stock in advance.
2. I'm _____ to analyze these surveys. I want to see how customers like our new services.
3. Is there a(n) _____ between rainy weather and lower sales?
4. Our computer _____ this morning. We can't respond to e-mails.
5. The server farm's security is _____. A card, password, and fingerprint scan are needed to get inside.

19

Reading Passage Track 9

In the Digital Age, massive amounts of data are **generated** every second. Internet searches, social media posts, GPS locations, and much more add up to what we call "big data." The information has positive uses, such as fighting disease and preventing crime. Yet, as with other advances, we have to be careful about its misuse.

Turning big data into actionable plans takes work. First, computers assign values to "structured" data (such as sales reports and database records) and "unstructured" data (such as e-mails, photos, and phone calls). These "data points" are analyzed using algorithms, artificial intelligence, and machine learning. The goal is to find **relationships** between data points and discover any patterns. That way, predictions can be made about what someone might buy or when equipment might **break down**.

The business world is a strong supporter of big data. Companies like Google and Facebook track and analyze our online activity. Later, we are shown ads for products that might interest us. As another example, equipment maker John Deere collects data from thousands of farms. Farmers share real-time details about fuel use, crop selections, and field conditions. Later, sets of "best practices" are made available to improve farmers' efficiency.

Public safety is another important area. For instance, Terra Seismic analyzes satellite data to **predict** earthquakes. With an **impressive** 90% **accuracy** rate, the company's work could save lives. In Los Angeles, the police department uses software to study crime patterns. Department resources are sent where needed. In places where the software is used, burglaries have fallen by 33%, and violent crimes have fallen by 21%.

Despite these successes, there are concerns, especially over privacy. "Data brokers" build and sell profiles about us, including our age, interests, and location. One company, Acxiom, has profiles of 500 million people. It's easy to imagine a future in which endless ads will target us.

Security is another concern. Computer breaches at firms like Yahoo have exposed the private information of hundreds of millions of people. That calls into question the safety of systems containing our personal details. Then there's the Internet of Things, which includes cars, phones, and other connected devices. They are also vulnerable to being hacked.

Corporations and governments are **eager** to put big data into action. A 2015 survey found that 63% of Fortune 1000 companies are already using it. They are cutting waste, lowering risk, and making smarter decisions. You and I also have a job. To protect ourselves, we need to understand how and by whom our personal information is being used.

> **Glossary**
> massive – very big; misuse – use in a bad way; actionable – able to be acted on; algorithm – formula or program used to act on data; crop – something (such as a type of fruit or vegetable) grown on a farm; efficiency – ability to operate without waste; burglary – theft from a building; profile – set of data describing a person or thing; breach – break in / hole; exposed – shown; vulnerable – having a weakness; corporation – large company; Fortune 1000 – list (made by *Fortune* magazine) of the largest American companies

Comprehension Check

Choose the best answer to each question.

Main Idea
1. What is the main idea?
   (A) Terra Seismic uses big data very successfully.
   (B) AI and machine learning are changing the way we do business.
   (C) Privacy in the age of big data is becoming rare.
   (D) Big data can be helpful or harmful, depending on how it's used.

Detail
2. Which of these uses of big data is NOT discussed in the article?
   (A) Making cities safer
   (B) Helping people work efficiently
   (C) Improving banking systems
   (D) Advertising products

Analysis
3. How is machine learning used with big data?
   (A) To collect information from customers
   (B) To analyze big data's privacy issues
   (C) To send e-mails to business managers
   (D) To find connections between data points

Circle if each statement is true (T) or false (F).

1. Acxiom is the LA police department's crime fighting software. (T / F)
2. Both structured and unstructured information are a part of big data. (T / F)

Vocabulary Check

A. Choose the best word or phrase to complete each sentence.

1. Our server _____ last night. That's why the website isn't working.
   (A) assigned values   (B) broke down   (C) lowered risk   (D) added up
2. We're _____ to start using these best practices as soon as possible.
   (A) personal   (B) massive   (C) important   (D) eager
3. By analyzing what you read and write online, companies can _____ what you will buy.
   (A) interest   (B) predict   (C) reduce   (D) prevent
4. There is a(n) _____ between the places we live and the clothes we wear.
   (A) information   (B) relationship   (C) government   (D) activity
5. The screen says it's 30 degrees in here, but everyone is cold. I'm worried about the _____ of the sensor.
   (A) accuracy   (B) supporter   (C) privacy   (D) profile

B. Choose the word that means the same as the underlined part.

1. The sales increase of 175% was called into question. Nobody could believe it.
   (A) doubted   (B) praised   (C) profited   (D) recorded
2. Google users generate an incredible amount of data every day.
   (A) create   (B) buy   (C) help   (D) read
3. The Internet of Things is full of impressive appliances like smart refrigerators.
   (A) expensive   (B) modern   (C) amazing   (D) necessary

Grammar Building - Noun Clauses

Circle the correct word to complete each sentence.

Ex: I'm not sure (where / that) the manual is.
Ans: I'm not sure *where* the manual is.

1. Can you tell me (where / which) the IT director went?
2. We're still learning (whichever / how) our customers' ages and spending habits are related.
3. The conference program has details about (what / how) the speakers will discuss.
4. (How / What) our sales grow isn't important. We just need them to improve.
5. I already told Gary (which / why) our server is having problems.

Grammar + Vocabulary

Put the words in the correct sentence order.

1. (will fly and / I predict / water one day / float on / that cars).
   _____

2. (might break down / can tell us / our trucks / Big data / when).
   _____

Technical Focus

A. Look at the diagram of the 5 Vs of big data. Then, circle if each statement is true (T) or false (F).

The 5 Vs of Big Data

- **Volume:** The data's quantity. The more, the better.
- **Value:** The data's goal. Big data is about creating value for an organization.
- **Veracity:** The data's cleanliness. Adding useful, problem-free data is important.
- **Velocity:** The data's speed. Real-time decisions require quick data processing.
- **Variety:** The type of data. Adding many data types can show hidden patterns.

1. The Value of big data refers to the speed of data processing. (T / F)
2. For more Variety, it's best to focus on just one kind of data. (T / F)
3. When businesses talk about data's Veracity, they are referring to its usefulness. (T / F)

B. Fill in the blanks with the correct word(s) from the box.

| to handle | thousands | although |
| even | requires | solution |

The analysis behind big data 1)_____ massive computing power. 2)_____ smaller companies may respect the 5 Vs, many don't have the resources to buy expensive computer systems. One 3)_____ is cloud computing. Specialty companies oversee giant server farms. They use software like Hadoop as well as 4)_____ of connected computers 5)_____ a job. Customers only pay when they need a task done. That way, 6)_____ small businesses can benefit from big data.

Word Parts

Study the word parts in the chart. Then, read the following pairs of sentences. Circle if the second sentence is true (T) or false (F).

Word Part	Meaning	Examples
dis-	apart	disease, distrust, distracting
-dict-	say / speak	predict, dictionary, contradict
-ful	full of	careful, helpful, forgetful

1. Carl's manager disagrees with his proposal to make the break room larger.
   They both feel the break room is already big enough. (T / F)

2. Everyone loves the colorful print in the lobby.
   The print is black and white. (T / F)

3. The personal assistant typed the letter as his boss dictated it.
   The boss spoke while the assistant typed. (T / F)

4. The storm's forceful winds knocked over hundreds of trees.
   The winds were calm, but heavy rain caused a lot of damage. (T / F)

5. For safety reasons, some scientists distrust computers with advanced AI.
   There are some scientists who do not trust the most modern versions of AI. (T / F)

Discussion

Discuss these questions with your classmates.

1. In some ways, using big data is like predicting the future. Are you comfortable with the idea of trying to see the future? Or are you against it? Why?

2. Some people try hard to keep their personal information private. Others are more public about their lives. They use social media websites like YouTube to tell the world about themselves. How about you? Are you very public, very private, or somewhere in the middle?

5 Rethinking Animal Intelligence

Track 10

Because we can't speak to animals, determining how smart they are is difficult. A new wave of research is helping us measure their intelligence. We are learning fascinating things about animals' social skills, their use of language, and more.

● Topic Warm-Up

Consider these statements. Circle if you agree (A) or disagree (D).

1. Some animals are very smart. (A / D)

2. We still have a lot to learn about animal behavior. (A / D)

● Vocabulary Warm-Up

Complete each sentence with the correct word or phrase. Remember to use the correct word form.

individual	aspect	ideally	achievement
native	determine	tend to	respect

1. We can _____ the age of a tree by counting its rings.
2. _____, there will be enough honey to fill 10 jars. That would be perfect.
3. I have a lot of _____ for Nikko's father. He knows everything about elephants.
4. The team won first place in the science contest. It was a big _____.
5. Are these flowers _____ to the area, or are they from somewhere else?

Reading Passage

Have you ever wondered what a dog or bird is thinking? There is a long history of speculation on the subject. Until recently, studies of animals have **tended to** compare their intelligence to that of humans. People are generally seen at the top of the intelligence scale, followed by chimpanzees, pigs, and so on. Thanks to new research techniques, these ranking concepts are losing favor. We're learning that land animals, marine life, and even insects have an impressive range of skills and brain functions.

Self-awareness is one measure of higher intelligence. For decades, a "mirror test" was used to **determine** if animals recognized themselves the way people can. Some, like apes, performed well. However, sight is just one sense, and many species have well-developed chemical detection abilities or other senses. For example, in 2017 a smell test was used to study how well dogs know their own scent. Their performance was excellent, and they even knew when another scent was added to their own. The findings suggested that when it comes to self-awareness, a dog's nose is more important than its eyes.

Language is another high-level skill. Many studies have been human-centered, such as teaching sign language to gorillas. New research methods are changing how we study this ability. For instance, a recent analysis of 90 species of dolphins, porpoises, and whales has shown cetaceans in a new light. Not only do dolphins talk to each other through whistles, but different groups have their own dialects. Besides that, unique calls are used for **individuals**. In other words, they have names. This use of language is just one **aspect** of cetaceans' complex social systems.

When it comes to social behavior, insects are gaining more **respect** for their **achievements**. Wasps, for example, know the difference between queens and workers. Plus, they share information and tasks to benefit the entire colony, not just individuals. We also now know that bees learn from each other. Younger bees observe how knowledgeable hive members fly to food sources. That behavior is copied, food is harvested more efficiently, and the colony's fortunes are improved.

Insect behavior, as well as that of whales, dogs, and other animals, has clear differences from that of humans. Scientists feel it is best to examine each species on its own merits. Instead of using tests designed for humans, we should study how animals behave in their **native** habitats. **Ideally**, intelligence should be a measure of a creature's ability to survive in its own social system and environment.

> **Glossary**
> speculation – wondering / guessing; lose favor – become less popular; marine – related to the ocean; impressive – excellent; self-awareness – being conscious of oneself; detection – knowing that something is present; scent – specific smell; sign language – using your hands to speak; cetacean – marine animal group containing dolphins, porpoises, and whales; dialect – local version of a language; colony – group of insects or animals; hive – place where bees live and make honey; harvest – gather something (ex: food); fortune – situation / luck; merit – good point; habitat – area where an animal, insect, etc. lives; creature – living being

Comprehension Check

Choose the best answer to each question.

Main Idea
1. What is the main idea?
    (A) The world's creatures are intelligent in ways that are different from people.
    (B) To learn about a species, we must study at least 90 individuals.
    (C) We don't know if marine animals are smarter than land animals.
    (D) Animals that use language or learn from each other are highly intelligent.

Detail
2. What is NOT true about dolphins' use of language?
    (A) There are clear language dialects from group to group.
    (B) Dolphins call each other by their names.
    (C) It's the only type of complex behavior shown by dolphins.
    (D) The cetaceans use whistles to speak.

Analysis
3. What is suggested about animals' abilities to recognize themselves?
    (A) It means they have some self-awareness.
    (B) Most animals use their eyes to recognize themselves.
    (C) Dogs perform the task better than people or apes.
    (D) They all use chemical detection skills.

Circle if each statement is true (T) or false (F).

1. Wasps know which individuals are workers and which are queens. (T / F)

2. Intelligence tests for people may not be suitable for understanding animals. (T / F)

Vocabulary Check

A. Choose the best word or phrase to complete each sentence.

1. Putting together the entire human genome was one of our top _____.
   (A) behaviors   (B) colonies   (C) creatures   (D) achievements

2. A pride of lions usually includes between 15 and 30 _____ living together.
   (A) individuals   (B) fortunes   (C) porpoises   (D) environments

3. The boat leaves in 10 minutes. _____, we'll see some whales.
   (A) As well as   (B) Ideally   (C) For instance   (D) Ever

4. Crows are known to use tools. It's just one _____ of their intelligence.
   (A) scent   (B) species   (C) aspect   (D) member

5. Recycling is a good way to show our _____ for the Earth.
   (A) measure   (B) respect   (C) ability   (D) detection

B. Choose the word that means the same as the underlined part.

1. I'm trying to determine how these parts fit together.
   (A) understand   (B) repair   (C) explain   (D) pretend

2. Once the river dried up, many native animals moved away.
   (A) local   (B) water   (C) hungry   (D) lost

3. Our dog doesn't like being cold, so she tends to stay indoors in the winter.
   (A) never   (B) rarely   (C) usually   (D) always

Grammar Building - Gerunds vs. Infinitives

Circle the correct word(s) to complete each sentence.

Ex: Chimpanzees use sticks (gathering / to gather) insects to eat.
Ans: Chimpanzees use sticks *to gather* insects to eat.

1. Bald eagles are skilled at (building / to build) large nests.
2. It takes the wolf several days (crossing / to cross) its habitat.
3. Some people enjoy (listening / to listen) to the sounds of rainforests.
4. My cat fell asleep after he finished (playing / to play) outside.
5. An elephant needs (eating / to eat) more than 100 kg of food every day.

Grammar + Vocabulary

Put the words in the correct sentence order.

1. (the meaning / will take time / Determining / dolphin whistle / of every).

   _____

2. (and animals / to respect / us / Biologists want / all plants).

   _____

Technical Focus

A. Look at the illustration of a dolphin and fish. Then, circle if each statement is true (T) or false (F).

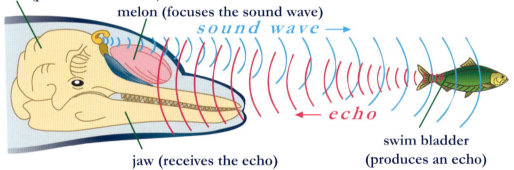

brain (processes the echo)
melon (focuses the sound wave)
sound wave →
← echo
jaw (receives the echo)
swim bladder (produces an echo)

1. The sound wave and echo move in the same direction. (T / F)
2. The melon allows the dolphin to focus the sound wave. (T / F)
3. The dolphin's swim bladder processes the echo. (T / F)

B. Fill in each blank with the correct word from the box.

make	even	called
ocean	by	object

Whistling is just one use of sound 1)_____ dolphins. Deep in the 2)_____, where there is little or no light, dolphins also use sound to see. The technique is 3)_____ "echolocation." Dolphins 4)_____ clicking noises to send out sound waves. After a sound wave bounces off an 5)_____ (such as a fish), its echo returns to the dolphin. The dolphin then knows the object's size, shape, location, and 6)_____ its speed.

Word Parts

Study the word parts in the chart. Then, read the following pairs of sentences. Circle if the second sentence is true (T) or false (F).

Word Part	Meaning	Examples
bene-	well / properly	benefit, benefactor, beneficial
-gen-	origin / kind / birth	generally, gender, regenerate
-age	related to / belonging to	language, wattage, passage

1. I watched a YouTube video about the genesis of the universe.
   The video was about the beginning of the universe. (T / F)

2. Being around adult baboons is beneficial for the young baboon's growth.
   As the young baboon grows, it's good for him to be near adults. (T / F)

3. The zoologists want to determine the percentage of sea otters that use tools.
   They are figuring out how many sea otters out of 100 use tools. (T / F)

4. In the park, there's little signage explaining the trees and flowers.
   You can see many signs telling you about the park's plant life. (T / F)

5. We use the instrument to generate an electrical pulse.
   The instrument's purpose is to stop the flow of electricity. (T / F)

Discussion

Discuss these questions with your classmates.

1. What are the most important measures of intelligence? (ex: language, using tools, etc.)

2. In your opinion, which animals are the smartest? Why?

6 Getting Chipped

Track 12

It has been suggested that computers will one day merge with humans. When that happens, we will have robotic body parts and attachments. In a way, the process has already begun. For various reasons, people are choosing to have microchips placed inside their bodies.

Topic Warm-Up

Consider these statements. Circle if you agree (A) or disagree (D).

1. Most advances in technology make our lives better. (A / D)
2. If it's useful, I might accept having a microchip implanted under my skin. (A / D)

Vocabulary Warm-Up

Complete each sentence with the correct word or phrase. Remember to use the correct word form.

| reality | emit | typically | long-term |
| perform | take note | passive | procedure |

1. The _____ to set his broken arm will take 20 minutes.
2. Some alarms _____ a very loud noise.
3. We'd better _____ of where we are. I don't want to get lost.
4. Rain storms in the valley _____ last two or three hours.
5. Steven is smart, but he's a little _____. He doesn't talk much unless someone asks him a question.

31

Reading Passage

We carry electronics everywhere. There are cell phones in our pockets and computers in our bags. How would you feel about having a microchip implanted inside your body? What may sound like science fiction is now a **reality**. As more people are choosing to get "chipped," privacy and healthcare professionals are raising concerns.

The **procedure** for implanting a microchip is fast and simple. Just the size of a grain of rice, the chip is usually inserted between a person's thumb and index finger. Chips **typically** contain simple information, such as a string of numbers, which is transmitted via RFID technology.

Here's how it works. When a chip is within a few centimeters of a sensor, it **emits** information via a radio wave. The sensor reads the data, which can be analyzed by software. A chipped person can also **perform** actions. They may include opening doors, buying things, and logging onto a computer, all done conveniently and quickly.

The first person to have a chip implanted into his body was Professor Kevin Warwick of Reading University. In 1998, he had the procedure done to help him study intelligent buildings. Since then, thousands of people in Mexico, Australia, the USA, and elsewhere have been chipped. Sweden has embraced the technology, which is used at offices, gyms, and train stations.

The medical field has also **taken note**. In 2004, the US Food and Drug Administration approved the use of Applied Digital Solutions' VeriChip for medical uses. The chip contains a 16-digit number that is linked to a patient's records. The hope is that the VeriChip will lead to fewer mistakes and better healthcare.

There are, to be sure, strong criticisms. One is that chipped people could be monitored by companies or governments. However, today's implanted chips do not have a power source, nor do they use GPS. They are "**passive**," remaining dormant until they are close to a sensor. In contrast, cell phones contain much more personal information, and they are easily tracked.

35 A second concern is over health issues. In some cases, animals with implants have developed tumors near the chips. There's a clear need for research into the **long-term** risks of leaving a chip inside your body for years.

Whatever your position is, the use of biometric devices is on the rise.
40 That includes fingerprint, facial, and iris recognition. Hackers have found such devices easy targets. If RFID chips are loaded with more personal data, they might face similar attacks. Therefore, it's important that security and safety continue to develop alongside the technology.

> **Glossary**
> implanted – placed inside; chipped – having an attached or implanted microchip; index finger – the finger next to your thumb; transmitted – sent; RFID – radio-frequency identification; embraced – welcomed; to be sure – certainly; monitored – watched and followed; dormant – asleep / inactive; tumor – irregular cell growth; position – opinion; biometric – involving the scanning of a part of one's body; iris – the colorful part of one's eye

Comprehension Check

Choose the best answer to each question.

Main Idea
1. What is the main idea?
    (A) Several interesting companies are making RFID chips and sensors.
    (B) Microchips cannot be felt or seen after they are implanted.
    (C) Implanted microchips are useful, but there are worries about them.
    (D) Professor Warwick underwent the first chip implant procedure.

Detail
2. Which of these uses of implanted chips is NOT discussed?
    (A) Turning on cell phones   (B) Paying for something
    (C) Accessing patient data   (D) Opening a door

Analysis
3. Why can't we monitor people who have implanted RFID chips?
    (A) Such chips must be very close to a sensor to transmit a signal.
    (B) RFID chips have a low-energy power source.
    (C) GPS doesn't work well in places that are far from city centers.
    (D) Users can block the scan by wearing gloves.

Circle if each statement is true (T) or false (F).

1. The VeriChip was designed to make it easier to enter offices and train stations. (T / F)

2. Everyone in the healthcare field believes implanted chips are safe. (T / F)

● Vocabulary Check

A. Choose the best word or phrase to complete each sentence.
1. The _____ for analyzing the data requires special software.
   (A) centimeter   (B) fingerprint   (C) procedure   (D) criticism
2. Please _____ of the chip sensor to the right of the door.
   (A) link to   (B) log onto   (C) take note   (D) load with
3. Some companies are giving employees a choice about getting chipped. In _____, many workers do not like the idea and are saying, "No, thank you."
   (A) target   (B) position   (C) device   (D) reality
4. Currently, the chips used by our employees do simple things like opening doors. The _____ plan is to have them linked to everything an employee does.
   (A) long-term   (B) alongside   (C) nearby   (D) everywhere
5. Rather than being quiet and _____, the boss wants us to state our opinions and make suggestions.
   (A) approved   (B) passive   (C) medical   (D) important

B. Choose the word or phrase that means the same as the underlined part.
1. The actions <u>performed</u> by an implanted chip are similar to those of a stored value card.
   (A) copied   (B) saved   (C) learned   (D) done
2. When it's safe to cross the street, the speaker <u>emits</u> a beeping sound.
   (A) sends out   (B) listens for   (C) takes in   (D) picks up
3. <u>Typically</u>, it only takes a few seconds to have a microchip implanted.
   (A) Usually   (B) Strangely   (C) Quickly   (D) Fortunately

● Grammar Building - Determiners

Circle the correct word to complete each sentence.

Ex: The system is neither good (or / nor) bad. Everything depends on how it's used.
Ans: The system is neither good *nor* bad. Everything depends on how it's used.

1. Both train stations (or / and) gyms in Sweden let people enter by scanning RFID chips.
2. You can choose either your right (or / nor) left hand to receive the implant.
3. Unfortunately, (either / neither) this tool nor that one will work for the job.
4. It's important that chip users feel (both / either) safe and comfortable.
5. Would (either / neither) a fingerprint reader or an iris scanner make the office more secure?

Grammar + Vocabulary

Put the words in the correct sentence order.

1. (radio signals / both emits / device / and receives / The).

   _____

2. (the recovery / is difficult / the medical procedure nor / Neither / process).

   _____

Technical Focus

A. Look at the illustration of a VeriChip implant. Then, circle if each statement is true (T) or false (F).

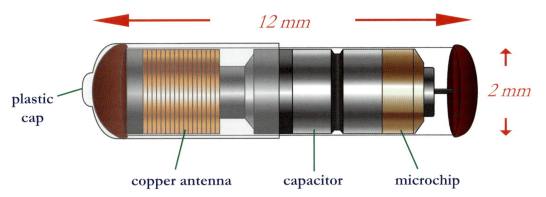

1. The microchip is surrounded by black wire. (T / F)
2. The capacitor is in between the microchip and the antenna. (T / F)
3. The whole unit is 12 mm long. (T / F)

B. Fill in the blanks with the correct word(s) from the box.

| to | information | the |
| contain | move around | there's |

Despite their size, VeriChip implants 1)_____ several working parts. A tiny capacitor is connected 2)_____ an antenna, forming a circuit. Power is supplied by the copper antenna when 3)_____ unit is near a reader. 4)_____ also an ID microchip. The radio signal that it generates contains 128 bits of 5)_____. Covering the whole unit is a special plastic cap. It bonds with human tissue so the device doesn't 6)_____ inside your body.

Word Parts

Study the word parts in the chart. Then, read the following pairs of sentences. Circle if the second sentence is true (T) or false (F).

Word Part	Meaning	Examples
micro-	very small	microchip, microscope, microphone
-mit-	send	transmit, submit, committed
-logy	related to a field	technology, geology, sociology

1. Jack is going to submit the report tomorrow.
   Tomorrow, Jack will receive the report. (T / F)

2. The virus which is causing the sickness is microscopic.
   To see the virus, you need to use special equipment. (T / F)

3. This anthropology book has an interesting article about the Mayans.
   Part of the book is about the Mayan people. (T / F)

4. Dr. Tanaka will use a micrometer to measure the length.
   The distance that Dr. Tanaka will measure is very large. (T / F)

5. Even when it's far from land, the boat can transmit a message using radio waves.
   The boat uses radio waves to send information. (T / F)

Discussion

Discuss these questions with your classmates.

1. After reading about implanted chips, how do you feel about them? Is it a positive technology? Is it negative? Or is it a bit of both?

2. In the future, people may receive more enhancements. For example, special suits could make us super strong. Chips in our brains could make us extra smart. What robotic enhancements can you imagine seeing in 50 or 100 years?

7 New Advances in Architecture

Track 14

Automation and 3D printing are influencing many fields, including architecture. Innovations are making construction work faster, less expensive, and more flexible. This new age of architecture is being led by creative people in companies of every size.

Topic Warm-Up

Consider these statements. Circle if you agree (A) or disagree (D).

1. If you want to design something special, it's best to work at a large company. (A / D)
2. I would like to live in a home that can be moved from place to place. (A / D)

Vocabulary Warm-Up

Complete each sentence with the correct word or phrase. Remember to use the correct word form.

| creative | innovation | factory | shave…off |
| appeal to | precisely | patented | construction |

1. Pressing this button releases _____ 5 ml of the liquid.
2. If we take this road, we'll _____ 10 minutes _____ our travel time.
3. The new cell phones _____ people who love video games.
4. My dad works at a(n) _____ that makes 600 refrigerators per day.
5. _____ people help companies think up ideas for new products.

37

Reading Passage Track 15

Architecture and the **construction** industry influence all of our lives. Careful planning goes into the structures we work, live, and study in. Recent advances in building design are using a blend of the latest technology and brilliant engineering. That's making it possible to create a diverse range of homes and offices which are flexible, affordable, and even mobile.

Some of the best **innovations** are coming from young firms like UK-based Ten Fold Engineering. The company, founded in 2011, designs structures which basically build themselves. Packages that look like long boxes are delivered by truck. With the press of a button, a **patented** lever system unfolds the home, store front, or other structure to three times its original size. It only takes 10 minutes, and a simple electric drill secures the building in place. If necessary, the building can be compacted again in just a few minutes and moved to another location. These masterpieces of engineering are built to last many years, and they can even be stacked on top of each other.

Speaking of stacking, that's an important part of the fast-growing modular construction field. Modular buildings consist of a number of smaller units, called modules, which are made at a **factory**. At the construction site, they are stacked on top of each other by cranes. Marriott, the world's largest hotel business, has been building hotels this way since 2016. Each module contains one hallway and two rooms with beds, sheets, chairs, and everything else inside. Once at the construction site, the electrical wiring and plumbing are completed. Thanks to this technique, Marriott is reducing costs, **shaving** months **off** construction schedules, and improving quality control.

When it comes to affordability and flexibility, 3D printing is also impacting the field. San Francisco-based Apis Cor has invented a mobile 3D printer that works wonders. With the appearance of a crane, it **precisely** releases a concrete mixture one layer at a time. In 2017, the apparatus was used to print the walls of a 37-square-meter home in just 24 hours. Then a roof, windows, and wiring were added. Although the total cost was only $10,134, the structure could last an incredible 175 years.

Such building solutions have endless possibilities. They include disaster relief, low-cost housing, and even robot-guided construction on other planets. These efficient, eco-friendly innovations **appeal to** people who value mobility. They are also proof that there's plenty of room for **creative** architects and engineers to redesign the world around us.

> **Glossary**
> structure – building; brilliant – very smart; flexible – changeable; affordable – not too expensive; drill – tool for making holes; compact – make smaller; masterpiece – top work / great achievement; modular – made of parts that fit together; stack – place on top of something; crane – machine used to lift and move things; plumbing – pipes and fixtures used to move water and waste; impact – influence; work wonders – do something amazing; concrete – a type of very strong building material; apparatus – device; endless – without limit; disaster – terrible event (ex: earthquake)

Comprehension Check

Choose the best answer to each question.

Main Idea
1. What is the main idea?
   (A) Home buyers and business owners want structures that can be quickly built.
   (B) New architectural methods benefit from good technology and smart design.
   (C) Engineers and architects are already thinking about buildings in deep space.
   (D) Workers will lose their jobs if 3D printers do more construction work.

Detail
2. How long does it take a Ten Fold Engineering building to unfold?
   (A) 10 minutes   (B) 24 hours   (C) 37 days   (D) 175 years

Analysis
3. What is suggested about the house made by Apis Cor?
   (A) All of the construction was done at a factory.
   (B) The wiring was done before the 3D printing began.
   (C) Some work was needed after the walls were finished.
   (D) Several cranes were used to complete the job.

Circle if each statement is true (T) or false (F).

1. Once you secure one of Ten Fold Engineering's buildings, it cannot be moved again. (T / F)

2. There are two furnished guest rooms and a hallway inside each Marriott module. (T / F)

● Vocabulary Check

A. Choose the best word or phrase to complete each sentence.

1. The _____ contains robots that make things while people monitor the process.
   (A) schedule   (B) factory   (C) disaster   (D) engineer
2. Small homes _____ people who want a simple life.
   (A) appeal to   (B) expect to   (C) use to   (D) bring to
3. Because the crane design is _____, other companies can't use it.
   (A) patented   (B) endless   (C) affordable   (D) guided
4. Look at this _____ piece of furniture. You can use it as a table, sofa, or bed.
   (A) electrical   (B) creative   (C) expected   (D) disastrous
5. The car's main _____ is its ability to park itself.
   (A) structure   (B) package   (C) appearance   (D) innovation

B. Choose the word that means the same as the underlined part.

1. Construction of the music hall is expected to be completed next spring.
   (A) Reading   (B) Applying   (C) Hiring   (D) Building
2. Using plastic instead of tin will shave 15% off production costs.
   (A) replace   (B) apply   (C) improve   (D) reduce
3. Painting one room takes precisely 2.5 hours.
   (A) suddenly   (B) exactly   (C) generally   (D) separately

● Grammar Building - Prepositions

Circle the correct word to complete each sentence.

Ex: Advances (in / to / out) chip design are making computers faster and more powerful.
Ans: Advances *in* chip design are making computers faster and more powerful.

1. You can start the car with the press (in / at / of) a button.
2. The cover is held (above / through / in) place by strong ropes.
3. The door handle is made of a blend (on / over / of) three metals.
4. Our firm is divided (into / onto / to) seven departments, including sales, planning, and so on.
5. We completed the design project (on / at / in) two months.

Grammar + Vocabulary

Put the words in the correct sentence order.

1. (have / the workers / the factory / All of / arrived at).

   _____

2. (construction projects / is used / patented mixture / for / The).

   _____

Technical Focus

A. Look at the illustration of an Apis Cor 3D printer. Then, circle if each statement is true (T) or false (F).

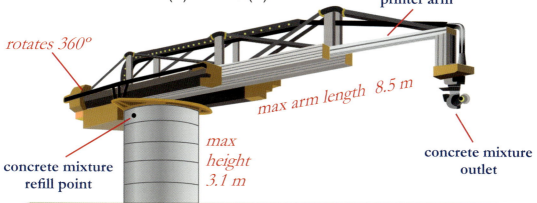

1. The printer's arm can reach a maximum length of 8.5 m. (T / F)
2. The printer can move up and down, but it cannot rotate. (T / F)
3. The concrete mixture refill point is located at the end of the printer's arm. (T / F)

B. Fill in the blanks with the correct word from the box.

machine	besides	easily
excellent	builds	that

The Apis Cor 3D printer has several 1)_____ features. It can 2)_____ be moved by truck to a building site. Only two people are needed to operate the printer as it 3)_____ a house around itself. 4)_____ being fast, it is incredibly efficient. The 5)_____ uses very little electricity, and it creates zero waste. The walls 6)_____ it builds are smooth, even, and strong.

41

Word Parts

Study the word parts in the chart. Then, read the following pairs of sentences. Circle if the second sentence is true (T) or false (F).

Word Part	Meaning	Examples
di-	apart / double / two	diverse, division, dioxide
-fac-	make / construct	factory, fact, factor
-eer	person involved with something	engineer, auctioneer, volunteer

1. All of the wheels are manufactured in Italy.
   Italy is the place where the wheels are made. (T / F)

2. Marty and Phillip enjoyed listening to the interesting dialogue.
   They listened to one person giving a speech. (T / F)

3. Gregory is a pamphleteer in his spare time.
   He spends some time making pamphlets. (T / F)

4. The knife is an ancient artifact from India.
   It's something that was written about but never made. (T / F)

5. The road will diverge in three kilometers.
   It's going to separate into different directions. (T / F)

Discussion

Discuss these questions with your classmates.

1. It's becoming faster, easier, and more affordable to build structures anywhere. What could be some good uses for these innovations? (ex: building a temporary clinic or schoolroom)

2. Because of advances in technology, more construction work is being done by machines. Fewer people are needed for construction jobs. In your opinion, what is good and bad about this change?

8 Making Science Popular: The Brilliance of Carl Sagan

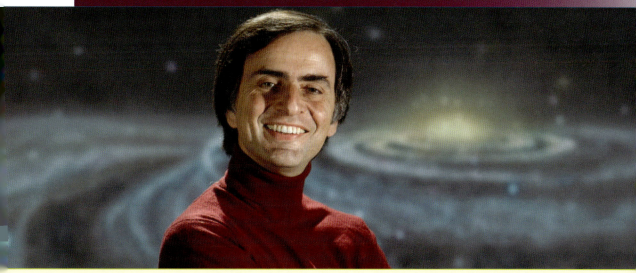

Track 16

In recent decades, astronomers have learned a great deal about the universe. However, their findings are sometimes technical and hard to explain. That's why we need scientists like Carl Sagan. He made topics like astronomy understandable and interesting to millions of people.

● Topic Warm-Up

Consider these statements. Circle if you agree (A) or disagree (D).

1. Part of a scientist's job should be explaining his or her findings to the public. (A / D)
2. Astronomers who appear on TV raise interest in space-related topics. (A / D)

● Vocabulary Warm-Up

Complete each sentence with the correct word or phrase. Remember to use the correct word form.

| knowledge | passionate | solar system | open mind |
| inspire | propose | brilliant | astronomer |

1. After reading about the 1969 moon landing, Charlotte was _____ to join a club that builds rockets.
2. Some scientists are so _____ about their research that they work nights and weekends.
3. I know you rarely watch science fiction movies, but keep a(n) _____. You might like this one.
4. Every year, _____ are learning more about space.
5. There aren't enough telescopes for everyone. What do you _____ we do?

43

Reading Passage Track 17

Our lives are enriched by science and its discoveries. Sometimes, though, the gap between research labs and the general public feels as vast as the Milky Way. It's fortunate that some of the greatest scientific minds have helped bridge that gap. Carl Sagan was one such man. He was a teacher,
5   **astronomer**, author, and TV star. Sagan has been called the most gifted scientific messenger of his time.

Carl Sagan was born in New York on November 9, 1934. Science was part of his life from an early age, and he loved reading
10   novels about space. Sagan worked hard on his education, earning multiple degrees (including a PhD) from the University of Chicago. In 1968, he took a teaching position at Cornell University, which
15   he held for the rest of his life. A popular teacher, he was known for encouraging students in their schoolwork and career plans.

In the 1960s, the young astronomer made important discoveries in planetary science. He **proposed** that the surface of Venus was made super-hot by a "greenhouse effect." Mars and Jupiter were two other
20   planets that he studied. To further stretch our **knowledge** of the **solar system**, Sagan worked with NASA. He was a consultant on the Mariner 2 mission to Venus and the Viking mission to Mars, among others. He was even involved with the famous plaques and records that were attached to the Pioneer and Voyager space probes.

25   Sagan was **passionate** about making science understandable to a wider audience. It helped that he was skilled at explaining complex ideas. In the 1970s, he discussed science topics on TV talk shows and wrote articles for popular magazines like *TV Guide*. Sagan became a worldwide superstar in 1980. That year, he hosted the TV show *Cosmos*, which he created with his
30   wife Ann Druyan. Its 13 episodes covered topics like the speed of light, the Voyager probes, and the search for alien life.

The show and its companion book (also called *Cosmos*) opened the eyes of hundreds of millions of people to the marvels of space. Another fascinating work was *Contact*, a science fiction novel that later became a movie. The
35   **brilliant** thinker wrote many more books, papers, and essays on space,

evolution, and other topics. Sadly, he died on December 20, 1996. During his years on our planet, Carl Sagan **inspired** a generation. He encouraged us to explore our shared future with an **open mind**, a sense of reason, and a feeling of wonder.

> **Glossary**
> enrich – improve / deepen; gap – separating distance; vast – wide; Milky Way – the galaxy we live in; bridge a gap – make a connection; gifted – talented; greenhouse effect – situation in which the sun's heat is trapped by gases in a planet's atmosphere; consultant – person who gives advice to a company, government, etc.; plaque – sign; probe – something sent out to gather information; companion – one thing that goes with something else; open someone's eyes – show or teach someone; evolution – biological change over time (ex: by an animal species)

Comprehension Check

Choose the best answer to each question.

Main Idea
1. What is the main idea?
   (A) As a writer and TV star, Carl Sagan interested millions of people in science.
   (B) The 1970s were a very busy time for Carl Sagan, but he enjoyed his work.
   (C) Some of Carl Sagan's colleagues were unhappy that he wrote for *TV Guide*.
   (D) To be as successful as Carl Sagan takes hard work and a passion for science.

Detail
2. Which of these achievements made Sagan famous worldwide?
   (A) His work on the Viking probes of Mars
   (B) His study of the temperature of Venus
   (C) His PhD work at the University of Chicago
   (D) His hosting of the TV show *Cosmos*

Analysis
3. What does the article suggest about Sagan's writings?
   (A) They were all about planetary science.
   (B) He wanted them to be easily read by a large audience.
   (C) Sagan wrote more books than essays.
   (D) *Contact* was both his longest and most popular book.

Circle if each statement is true (T) or false (F).

1. Carl Sagan first became interested in space at the University of Chicago. (T / F)

2. Carl Sagan studied several planets, including Venus and Jupiter. (T / F)

Vocabulary Check

A. Choose the best word or phrase to complete each sentence.

1. _____ use tools on Earth and in space to examine the stars.
   (A) Interests   (B) Astronomers   (C) Discoveries   (D) Episodes
2. Daniel is a _____ speaker, waving his arms and talking loudly while giving speeches.
   (A) reasonable   (B) passionate   (C) planetary   (D) companion
3. If you don't have a(n) _____, it's hard to accept other people's ideas.
   (A) science fiction   (B) early warning   (C) open mind   (D) general public
4. In our _____, Mercury is the closest planet to the sun.
   (A) solar system   (B) wide audience
   (C) complex idea   (D) greenhouse effect
5. A good teacher can _____ his or her students to do great things with their lives.
   (A) explain   (B) wonder   (C) create   (D) inspire

B. Choose the word that means the same as the underlined part.

1. After Albert Einstein's death, some of the theories that he <u>proposed</u> were shown to be correct.
   (A) suggested   (B) borrowed   (C) doubted   (D) allowed
2. <u>Brilliant</u> thinkers sometimes come from the poorest places. That's one reason everyone deserves a good education.
   (A) Intelligent   (B) Respected   (C) Educated   (D) Wealthy
3. Scholars who focus on one area develop a deep <u>knowledge</u> of the field.
   (A) questioning   (B) reporting   (C) programming   (D) understanding

Grammar Building - The Passive Voice

Circle the correct word to complete each sentence.

Ex: The lecture was (gave / given) by the geologist after her visit to Australia.
Ans: The lecture was *given* by the geologist after her visit to Australia.

1. Carl Sagan dictated his books and articles into a tape recorder. They were then (type / typed) up by assistants.
2. Will the rocket launch be (showed / shown) on TV?
3. No, I don't think the conference schedule has been (post / posted) yet.
4. The interview was (held / hold) at the chemist's laboratory.
5. The rules of the robot competition will be (announce / announced) tomorrow.

Grammar + Vocabulary

Put the words in the correct sentence order.

1. (has been / in great detail / solar system / studied / Our).

   _____

2. (to become / Carl Sagan / scientists / were inspired by / Many children).

   _____

Technical Focus

A. Look at the illustration of the Golden Record's cover. Then, circle if each statement is true (T) or false (F).

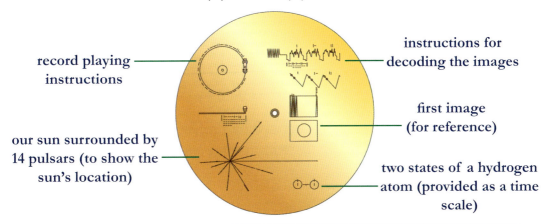

1. The cover's directions are in three languages. (T / F)
2. The image decoding instructions are beneath the record playing instructions. (T / F)
3. Hydrogen atoms are shown in order to provide a time scale. (T / F)

B. Fill in the blanks with the correct word(s) from the box.

| called | by | was included |
| how | into | languages |

The Voyager 1 and 2 probes, launched 1)_____ space in 1977, each contained a copy of a special item 2)_____ the "Golden Record." It 3)_____ in case an intelligent alien species finds one of the probes. On the Golden Record are numerous recordings, including sounds of nature, music 4)_____ Beethoven, Chuck Berry's song "Johnny B. Goode," and much more. There are also greetings in 55 5)_____. And there are 115 pictures, recorded as a series of signals. The record's cover gives directions on 6)_____ to use it.

● Word Parts

Study the word parts in the chart. Then, read the following pairs of sentences. Circle if the second sentence is true (T) or false (F).

Word Part	Meaning	Examples
super-	beyond / above / over	superstar, superior, supernatural
-sol-	sun	solar system, solstice, parasol
-able	possible / able	understandable, readable, doable

1. Solar panels work best in open areas where there are no trees in the way.
   It's important that the sun is not blocked. (T / F)

2. Lake Wilkinson isn't reachable by car.
   It might be possible to drive to the lake. (T / F)

3. The students' work will be supervised by Professor Tezuka.
   The professor will oversee what the students are doing. (T / F)

4. Their sickness is treatable with medicine.
   Doctors are not sure what to do about the problem. (T / F)

5. Jacob believes there is a supernatural power making the strange noises.
   According to Jacob, the noises are from a natural source like a river. (T / F)

● Discussion

Discuss these questions with your classmates.

1. One of Carl Sagan's interests was the search for alien life. Do you believe there is life on other planets? If so, do you think the aliens are friendly or dangerous?

2. Sagan used the media of his time, including print and television, to reach people. These days, what's the best way to spread a message to the largest number of people?

9 Extreme Weather and Climate Change

Track 18

Climate change is typically associated with rising temperatures. Global warming is serious, but it isn't the only result of the crisis. There is growing evidence that climate change is also linked to stronger hurricanes, larger floods, and other extreme weather events.

Topic Warm-Up

Consider these statements. Circle if you agree (A) or disagree (D).

1. Recently, I've noticed an increase in the number of large storms. (A / D)
2. Problems like rising sea levels make me worried about living near the ocean. (A / D)

Vocabulary Warm-Up

Complete each sentence with the correct word. Remember to use the correct word form.

humid	extreme	majority	blame
warning	likewise	absorb	simulation

1. The rise in fruit prices was _____ on the floods which damaged farmlands.
2. My classmates and I are going to plant trees this weekend. _____, my mom and dad are joining a tree-planting group.
3. The _____ of scientists agree that human activity is causing global warming.
4. It feels so _____ outside. I wonder if it's going to rain.
5. There's a(n) _____ on the box. It says to keep the item away from children.

Reading Passage Track 19

Over the last century, the Earth has warmed by about 1° Celsius. Though it seems like a small number, we're already seeing dramatic changes to the climate. Record-high temperatures are being set every year. There has also been an increase in **extreme** weather events like heat waves, droughts, and floods.

Scientists don't **blame** every weather event on climate change, but there is a growing consensus that it is making things worse. One tool to study this link is "attribution science." After a hurricane, for example, a computerized weather model is built. Researchers remove the effects of global warming from the model and run a **simulation**. If the result is different, it shows a link between climate change and the event.

Heat waves lasting days or weeks are clearly associated with global warming. In fact, record highs are becoming commonplace. In 2017 the US cities of San Francisco and Phoenix hit records of 41° and 48°, respectively. A study in Europe gave a strong **warning** about the trend. If global warming reaches 3° by 2100, it could result in 152,000 yearly deaths in Europe. The great **majority** would be caused by heat waves.

Higher temperatures also lead to more serious droughts and wildfires. Because heat speeds up the evaporation of water from the soil, droughts continue even if it rains. That's what happened with Sao Paulo's recent drought, which lasted an incredible two years. **Likewise**, drier-than-normal forests experience more serious wildfires. For instance, in 2017 California suffered from large wildfires which killed dozens of people and burned thousands of homes.

The threat from extreme weather is not just land based. The ocean's surface temperature has risen an average of 0.56° since 1880. Warmer water makes storms more intense, worsening disasters like Hurricane Maria, which battered Puerto Rico. Warmer oceans also have higher evaporation rates, leading to a more **humid** atmosphere. That causes huge rainstorms and floods, such as those recently seen in India, Nepal, and Bangladesh. The loss of life in those disasters exceeded 1,500 people.

Efforts are underway to slow down global warming. The goal is to limit the temperature rise to 2° or less. Steps include using more wind power, solar power, and electric cars to reduce carbon emissions. Planting new forests, which **absorb** CO_2 from the air, is another positive step. Even with those moves, extreme weather will be with us for the near future. More efforts are therefore needed to protect countries from storms, heat waves, and other disasters.

> **Glossary**
> dramatic – serious; climate – general weather; drought – long period of dry weather; flood – water flowing over lands that are normally dry; consensus – agreement; attribution – placing responsibility on something; hurricane – large storm that starts in the ocean; associated with – related to; respectively – The first point refers to the first thing in a list. The second point refers to the second thing. etc.; wildfire – quickly spreading fire that is out of control; evaporation – the turning of water into a gas; soil – land / earth; intense – serious; batter – hit hard; exceed – be greater than

Comprehension Check

Choose the best answer to each question.

Main Idea
1. What is the main idea?
   (A) San Francisco and Phoenix hit record-high temperatures in 2017.
   (B) Climate change is worsening weather-related disasters.
   (C) Extreme weather events happen both on land and in the ocean.
   (D) We need to work harder to protect people from wildfires.

Detail
2. How much has the ocean's surface warmed since the late 19th century?
   (A) 0.56°   (B) 1°   (C) 2°   (D) 48°

Analysis
3. What does the article suggest about the near future?
   (A) There won't be any more droughts if we stop global warming.
   (B) Preventing flooding is the most important action we can take.
   (C) Every year, there will be a rise in the number of hurricanes.
   (D) We will see more serious weather events in the coming years.

Circle if each statement is true (T) or false (F).

1. Attribution science shows us if weather events are related to climate change. (T / F)

2. Droughts always end right after it starts raining. (T / F)

● Vocabulary Check

A. Choose the best word to complete each sentence.
1. Flight _____ help students learn to fly real airplanes.
   (A) temperatures (B) simulations (C) rainstorms (D) emissions
2. Please use this towel to _____ the water from the floor.
   (A) become (B) worsen (C) absorb (D) protect
3. Let's hear everyone's opinion. We'll let the _____ of our members decide where we go.
   (A) majority (B) century (C) climate (D) effort
4. The small firms don't have a lot of money. We shouldn't _____ them for not buying expensive machinery.
   (A) cause (B) blame (C) last (D) build
5. Rainforests are very _____ places. Even when it isn't raining, it feels wet.
   (A) strong (B) humid (C) solar (D) clear

B. Choose the word that means the same as the underlined part.
1. On days when the heat is extreme, it's wise to stay indoors.
   (A) serious (B) common (C) possible (D) unknown
2. Walking is one way to reduce carbon emissions. Likewise, using solar power in your home is helpful.
   (A) Somewhat (B) So (C) Maybe (D) Also
3. There's a big warning on the fence not to climb over it.
   (A) photo (B) lock (C) caution (D) wall

● Grammar Building - Adverb Clauses

Circle the correct word to complete each sentence.

Ex: Mark is wearing a jacket (after / although) it is hot outside.
Ans: Mark is wearing a jacket *although* it is hot outside.

1. Can you please check the weather forecast (before / so) we go out?
2. (As / Although) the river rose to dangerous levels, residents prepared to leave.
3. I'm on my way to the airport. I'll call you (whereas / after) I get there.
4. (Because / Before) the ocean is warmer than usual, the hurricane may be strong.
5. Miranda is using public transportation more often (though / since) she wants to help the environment.

Grammar + Vocabulary

Put the words in the correct sentence order.

1. (it's so / change shirts / humid / because / I want to).

   _____

2. (staying inside / extreme, we're / Since today's / will be / heat).

   _____

Technical Focus

A. Look at the illustration of a hurricane. Then, circle if each statement is true (T) or false (F).

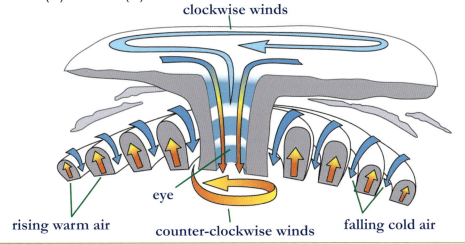

1. In a hurricane, warm air falls while cold air rises. (T / F)
2. The eye of the hurricane is in its center. (T / F)
3. The base of the storm moves in a clockwise direction. (T / F)

B. Fill in the blanks with the correct word(s) from the box.

| very | caused | strong storms |
| their | become | one of |

In recent years, huge Category 4 and 5 hurricanes have 1)_____ frequent. 2017 was a 2)_____ strong year. Hurricane Harvey 3)_____ huge floods in Texas. Mexico was hit hard by Hurricane Katia. And Hurricane Irma, 4)_____ the largest ever recorded, tore through the Caribbean and Florida. Coastal areas have always dealt with 5)_____. With rising ocean levels and larger hurricanes, the risks facing people and 6)_____ property are growing.

Word Parts

Study the word parts in the chart. Then, read the following pairs of sentences. Circle if the second sentence is true (T) or false (F).

Word Part	Meaning	Examples
con-	together / also	consensus, connect, contain
-cred-	belief	incredible, credential, discredit
-wise	same / in such a way	likewise, lengthwise, otherwise

1. To open the case, turn the handle clockwise.
   The handle should be turned in the same direction that a clock's hands move. (T / F)

2. Jack and the repairman concur that the window needs replacing.
   The two people have different opinions about the job. (T / F)

3. The data adds credence to scientists' warnings about rising sea levels.
   Because of the information, scientists' warnings are more believable. (T / F)

4. Please measure the box lengthwise and tell me the number.
   The person wants to know how long the box is. (T / F)

5. The report about aliens visiting the Earth is not credible.
   It is possible that the report is true. (T / F)

Discussion

Discuss these questions with your classmates.

1. Who is the most responsible for climate change: people, businesses, or governments?
2. What can we do in our daily lives to fight climate change?

10 Virtual Reality in Medicine

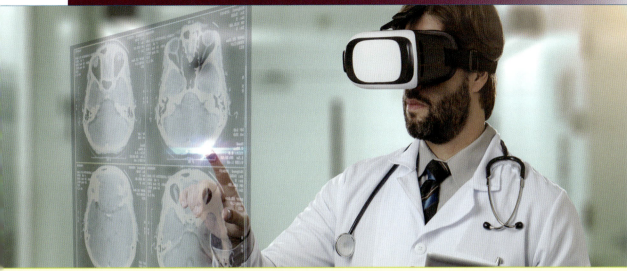

Track 20

Although virtual reality was invented decades ago, it's still usually thought of in terms of entertainment. Thanks to 3D scanning and other advances, the medical field has also made virtual reality an important tool. Its uses are growing every year.

Topic Warm-Up

Consider these statements. Circle if you agree (A) or disagree (D).

1. Virtual reality could be a powerful learning tool for medical students. (A / D)
2. Patients heal faster when they are relaxed and playing games. (A / D)

Vocabulary Warm-Up

Complete each sentence with the correct word or phrase. Remember to use the correct word form.

| effective | expand | victim | physical therapy |
| evidence | interact | operation | work wonders |

1. The Internet and mobile devices make it easy to _____ with anyone, anywhere.
2. After she broke her leg, Paula needed six weeks of _____.
3. The medical group runs three clinics. They want to _____ the number to five.
4. There's no _____ of who stole the equipment. The building doesn't have any cameras, and nobody saw anything.
5. Sergio's medicine _____. He felt better after just a few days.

55

Reading Passage

Through our eyes, we view the world in rich color and amazing detail. But there are limits to what we can see and where we can go. Enter virtual reality (VR). The technology **expands** our vision, providing countless entertainment, work, and travel possibilities. VR is also being successfully used in the medical field by students, doctors, and patients.

Becoming a doctor starts with years of education and training. To help with the process, USC's Medical Virtual Reality group created "Virtual Patient." Students **interact** with 3D characters to hone doctor/patient skills and diagnose conditions. Thanks also to VR, students don't have to be inside an operating room to study a doctor's techniques. In 2016, Professor Shafi Ahmed performed surgery on a cancer patient in London. Cameras created a 360 degree viewing angle, and the **operation** was watched by more than 13,000 medical students worldwide.

Surgery preparation is seeing benefits as well. EchoPixel has software that turns data from CT scans, X-rays, and MRIs into 3D images. At Masonic Children's Hospital, one such "3D visualization" was used to prepare for an operation to separate conjoined twins. Doctors wore VR headsets to examine the connections between the twins' hearts and livers. Problems were anticipated, and a plan was made, leading to a successful operation.

Patients are also using VR technology, which is especially helpful for those in pain. At the University of Washington, a program called Snow World was developed for burn **victims**. During bandage changes and other treatments, patients play a VR game in which they throw snowballs. The game distracts their brains from pain sensations. It **works wonders**, and pain reductions of up to 50% have been reported.

Physical therapy is another promising area. Swiss Mindmaze has a VR app that stroke victims use to practice lifting their arms. There is growing **evidence** that such tools are **effective**. A 2012 study of recovering stroke patients focused on video capture technology. During their therapy, half of the patients saw themselves on a screen inside a virtual world. The other half received standard therapy only. The study found that the patients using VR had higher levels of improvement.

Medical uses of this amazing technology are endless. They include treating phobias, improving the lives of bedridden patients, and much more. There's an old expression: "It's all in your head." In this case, that's a positive thing. VR lets us move beyond our restrictions, unlocking the power of our imagination. Most importantly, although the images that people see are digital, the healthcare outcomes are very real.

> **Glossary**
> virtual – digital / similar to the original thing; countless – endless; USC – University of Southern California; hone – sharpen; diagnose – figure out what is wrong; CT – computerized tomography; MRI – magnetic resonance imaging; visualization – image of something; conjoined twins – two people who are born with connected bodies; anticipated – planned for; distract – turn attention elsewhere; sensation – feeling; app – mobile application; stroke – condition in which blood stops flowing to the brain; phobia – fear; bedridden – unable to leave one's bed

Comprehension Check

Choose the best answer to each question.

Main Idea
1. What is the main idea?
   (A) For most types of VR, the user wears a headset.
   (B) By showing us what we can't normally see, VR is aiding the medical field.
   (C) Every stroke patient should use VR to recover faster.
   (D) Being inside the operating room isn't the only way to see a live operation.

Detail
2. Which group benefitting from VR is NOT discussed in the article?
   (A) Patients   (B) Hospital designers   (C) Doctors   (D) Medical students

Analysis
3. What does the article suggest about medical care?
   (A) Our imagination can be an important tool in helping us heal.
   (B) When someone doesn't feel well, he or she should get help right away.
   (C) Most hospitals in the UK show live operations online.
   (D) Students who use VR don't need to practice talking to real patients.

Circle if each statement is true (T) or false (F).

1. EchoPixel's software lets you talk to virtual characters. (T / F)
2. Playing Snow World helps burn victims think of something besides their pain. (T / F)

Vocabulary Check

A. Choose the best word or phrase to complete each sentence.

1. The accident _____ were rushed to the hospital within minutes.
   (A) outcomes   (B) victims   (C) headsets   (D) restrictions
2. Modern medicine _____ in ways that were once hard to imagine.
   (A) grows evidence   (B) creates angles
   (C) plays games   (D) works wonders
3. Nurse Kelly is great at _____ with patients and answering their questions.
   (A) promising   (B) receiving   (C) interacting   (D) including
4. Two doctors will perform the _____ to repair the man's knee.
   (A) operation   (B) imagination   (C) software   (D) condition
5. After three months of _____, Rita can finally walk again.
   (A) virtual world   (B) physical therapy
   (C) 3D images   (D) doctor/patient skills

B. Choose the word that means the same as the underlined part.

1. There is some evidence that thinking positively can help you heal faster.
   (A) medicine   (B) proof   (C) question   (D) response
2. The children's hospital is expanding its use of VR for seriously ill kids.
   (A) growing   (B) treating   (C) buying   (D) playing
3. VR headsets are effective in helping people imagine that they are on a beach.
   (A) successful   (B) relaxing   (C) healthy   (D) creative

Grammar Building - Parallel Structures

Choose the correct word to complete each sentence.

Ex: We'll check your blood pressure, take your pulse, and (measure / measuring) your temperature.
Ans: We'll check your blood pressure, take your pulse, and *measure* your temperature.

1. VR users enjoy playing games, (to talk / talking) with characters, and visiting new places.
2. After the operation, you may feel (tiring / tired), uncomfortable, and a little sick.
3. New treatments for (fears / fearfully), worries, and other issues are being developed.
4. The doctor said you need to rest, drink a lot of water, and (eat / to eat) well.
5. We can do the physical therapy in the room, (at / enjoy) the park, or by the lake.

Grammar + Vocabulary

Put the words in the correct sentence order.

1. (and effective / is a / diagnostic tool / quick, easy, / An MRI scan).

   _____

2. (victims of / This clinic / workplace accidents / treats / road, home, and).

   _____

Technical Focus

A. Look at the illustration of a VR game for stroke recovery. Then, circle if each statement is true (T) or false (F).

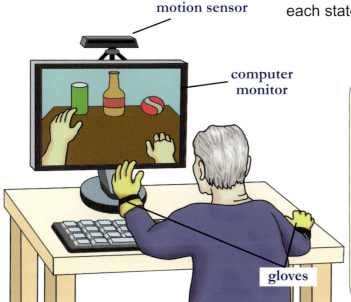

1. To play the game, the patient wears gloves on both hands. (T / F)

2. The motion sensor is on top of the monitor. (T / F)

3. On the screen, the patient only sees a pair of hands. (T / F)

B. Fill in the blanks with the correct word(s) from the box.

can be	up	kicking
more	developed	each

For stroke patients, learning to use one's arms or legs again 1)_____ difficult. Several VR games have been 2)_____ to speed up the process. In one game for building leg strength, patients see themselves 3)_____ a ball. In another for building hand strength, players see themselves picking things 4)_____. Games can be adjusted for 5)_____ patient's condition. Using gloves and a headset makes the experience even 6)_____ realistic.

Word Parts

Study the word parts in the chart. Then, read the following pairs of sentences. Circle if the second sentence is true (T) or false (F).

Word Part	Meaning	Examples
inter-	between	interact, interview, interior
-vis-	sight	visualization, advise, visit
-wide	of a certain size	worldwide, countrywide, citywide

1. The supermarket is having a storewide sale.
   There are discounted products in just one section of the store. (T / F)

2. Dr. Phillips is acting as an intermediary in the discussions.
   He is working between both sides in the talks. (T / F)

3. The monitor which is used for the VR program is visible from the patient's bed.
   You can see the monitor while lying in bed. (T / F)

4. Rasberry Hill is the place where the two roads intersect.
   The roads do not cross each other at Rasberry Hill. (T / F)

5. Before an operation, doctors use VR to visualize what might happen.
   Doctors use VR to see what could happen in the operating room. (T / F)

Discussion

Discuss these questions with your classmates.

1. In your opinion, which use of VR in the medical field is the most interesting? Why?

2. Some people are worried about VR. They think we will spend too much time using the technology. The fear is users may not want to return to the "real world." What do you think about that?

11 Should we fear intelligent machines?

Track 22   For a long time, humans have had the most powerful brains on Earth. That could soon change. Every year, machines are getting smarter and doing more complex tasks. Is that something we should fear? There are some interesting ideas about why we should or shouldn't be afraid.

● Topic Warm-Up

Consider these statements. Circle if you agree (A) or disagree (D).

1. Computers will be smarter than people in 20 years. (A / D)
2. I'm worried that intelligent machines may be dangerous. (A / D)

● Vocabulary Warm-Up

Complete each sentence with the correct word or phrase. Remember to use the correct word form.

| instantly | optimistic | raise an alarm | estimate |
| debate | rely on | behave | obsolete |

1. Millions of people _____ their cell phones for daily tasks. There is some concern that we may forget how to do things like basic math.
2. The carpenter's time _____ for finishing the repair is two weeks.
3. It's a very fast machine. When you hit the power button, it turns on _____.
4. My old computer isn't powerful enough to play those new games. It's already _____.
5. We're _____ about the software. We think it will be a big hit.

61

Reading Passage Track 23

Artificial intelligence (AI) is becoming a familiar part of daily life. Cell phones, call centers, and marketing campaigns are some of its many uses. Is there a danger in making machines too clever? What happens when they become smarter than people? As the technology marches towards super intelligence, some observers are **raising alarms**.

One concern is over jobs. White collar professionals like lawyers and accountants **rely on** years of education and experience to do their work. Imagine a computer that can **instantly** review every law to find the best defense. Such a system would make human lawyers **obsolete**. Tech executives like IBM's Jordan Bitterman remain **optimistic**. They feel that as AI expands, new jobs will be created.

Another concern is over safety. AI is currently used for "narrow" tasks such as recognizing faces. As their abilities grow, super-smart machines may handle advanced tasks like air traffic control systems. They could also rewrite their software or build other machines. At a conference in 2015, experts were asked when they thought computers would reach this point. The average **estimate** was 2045. What will machines do when they have such power?

That's the question worrying tech leaders like Elon Musk. Much of the **debate** is over morality. When a person does a job, he or she follows a value system. For example, we avoid hurting people, and we generally try to be fair. Machines, in contrast, are logic-driven, with a focus on reaching goals. Let's say a system's job is to build an apartment building. While doing so, it could pollute a river or hurt local wildlife. To avoid such problems, the system must first have a deep understanding of human values.

AI supporters like Facebook's Mark Zuckerberg see the technology as a positive force. They believe it will improve our lives in medicine, business, and elsewhere. The real danger, it's felt, is not computers but the people who program them. It's also felt that science fiction movies about evil robots spread false ideas. Without emotions, there's no reason for machines to turn against us.

At this time, scientists and engineers simply don't know how an advanced system will **behave**. That's why Musk founded OpenAI. The company is trying to develop AI in a safe and responsible way. There's also optimism when it comes to values. Computers could one day teach themselves about human cultures by studying books and other resources. Hopefully, with enough safeguards in place, we will have nothing to fear from intelligent machines.

> **Glossary**
> familiar – something we are used to seeing; marketing – selling and advertising; clever – smart; march – move / walk; white collar – related to an office job; accountant – person who gives advice about money, taxes, etc.; executive – high-level manager; air traffic – the airplanes currently in the sky; conference – event where people with the same work or interests meet; morality – sense of right and wrong; value – belief; pollute – make dirty; wildlife – animals in a natural setting; safeguard – something that improves safety

Comprehension Check

Choose the best answer to each question.

Main Idea
1. What is the main idea?
   - (A) We aren't sure what will happen once computers become super intelligent.
   - (B) As the use of AI spreads, a debate over its pros and cons is underway.
   - (C) When Mark Zuckerberg discusses AI, everyone pays close attention.
   - (D) OpenAI makes the software and hardware that run every AI system.

Detail
2. Which of the following is true about "narrow" computing tasks?
   - (A) Computers may start doing them in 2045.
   - (B) They are the tasks that people like Elon Musk are worried about.
   - (C) Building other machines is an example of a "narrow" task.
   - (D) AI systems can already perform such tasks.

Analysis
3. What is suggested about machines that learn about human values?
   - (A) They can never understand fairness since it's so complex.
   - (B) They may have a good reason to turn against people.
   - (C) They will be safe and make us less afraid of AI.
   - (D) They might be used by criminals to break the law.

Circle if each statement is true (T) or false (F).

1. White collar workers could lose their jobs to intelligent machines. (T / F)

2. Mark Zuckerberg feels AI has more positive than negative points. (T / F)

● Vocabulary Check

A. Choose the best word or phrase to complete each sentence.
1. There is a big _____ over whether the Internet is making us smarter or lazier.
   (A) lawyer   (B) safety   (C) debate   (D) power
2. Some people believe electronic products are designed to be _____ within a few years. That way, you have to keep buying new ones.
   (A) obsolete   (B) familiar   (C) general   (D) professional
3. Professor Harris _____ his assistants. They are of great help to his research.
   (A) relies on   (B) tries to   (C) marches towards   (D) turns against
4. My radio is _____ strangely. It keeps changing stations by itself.
   (A) improving   (B) behaving   (C) reviewing   (D) avoiding
5. The cost _____ for the hardware upgrade is lower than we expected.
   (A) conference   (B) accountant   (C) ability   (D) estimate

B. Choose the word or phrase that means the same as the underlined part.
1. The business leader raised an alarm. She advised everyone to keep up with digital trends if they want to keep their jobs.
   (A) returned a favor   (B) asked a question
   (C) gave a warning   (D) made a sale
2. When I saw Carly's face, I instantly knew she was upset.
   (A) so sadly   (B) by chance   (C) from afar   (D) very quickly
3. Do you feel optimistic about robots working as nurses and doctors?
   (A) healthy   (B) positive   (C) amazed   (D) afraid

● Grammar Building - Modals

Choose the correct word to complete each sentence.

Ex: I (might / will) attend the robotics conference. I'm not sure yet.
Ans: I *might* attend the robotics conference. I'm not sure yet.

1. You (must / may) remove your shoes before going inside. It's the rule.
2. I (can / can't) help you with your chemistry homework. I don't understand the subject.
3. The lecture (will / would) begin at 11:30. Please arrive a few minutes early.
4. Your lab results are fascinating. You (wouldn't / should) write a paper about them.
5. It (may / can) rain later today. Remember to bring an umbrella.

Grammar + Vocabulary

Put the words in the correct sentence order.

1. (to solve / rely on / You shouldn't / your problems / other people).

   _____

2. (a few years / will be / That computer model / obsolete / within).

   _____

Technical Focus

A. Look at the illustration of a Turing test. Then, circle if each statement is true (T) or false (F).

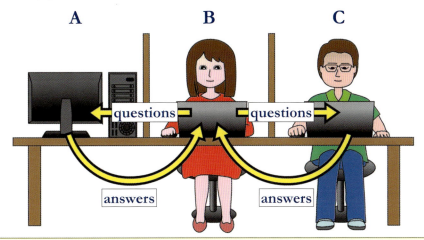

1. A, B, and C do not see each other when answering questions. (T / F)
2. During the test, A speaks out loud to C. (T / F)
3. The computer asks questions which are answered by two people. (T / F)

B. Fill in the blanks with the correct word(s) from the box.

ability	finally	using
by	conversations	think that

The Turing test was created 1)_____ Alan Turing in 1950. It tests a computer's 2)_____ to think. 3)_____ a keyboard, a tester has a "blind" chat with two respondents. One respondent is a person, and one is a machine. 4)_____ are held with many testers. The computer has to make 30% of the testers 5)_____ it is a real person. A machine 6)_____ passed the test in 2014.

Word Parts

Study the word parts in the chart. Then, read the following pairs of sentences. Circle if the second sentence is true (T) or false (F).

Word Part	Meaning	Examples
pro-	for / (put) forward	program, protect, provide
-mot-	move	emotion, motivation, remote
-er	person who does something	supporter, builder, thinker

1. Mr. Suzuki is a supporter of computer education for children.
   Mr. Suzuki believes in teaching kids about computers. (T / F)

2. Pete tried getting off the bus while it was in motion.
   The bus was stopped when Pete tried getting off. (T / F)

3. The parade will proceed even if the weather is bad.
   No matter what the weather is like, the parade will go forward. (T / F)

4. The non-profit group provides free computers to schools in poor countries.
   To increase profits, the group makes computers in countries where costs are low. (T / F)

5. Chika is the best regional manager we've ever had.
   Chika does a great job managing the area. (T / F)

Discussion

Discuss these questions with your classmates.

1. Are there some jobs that we should never give machines? If so, what are they?

2. In countries with aging populations, intelligent machines may soon care for older people. How do you feel about that?

12 Megacities

Track 24

Cities are the world's economic and cultural centers. Because so many people are moving to urban areas, we are seeing the growth of more "megacities." These population centers provide good jobs and other benefits, but they also have oversized problems.

Topic Warm-Up

Consider these statements. Circle if you agree (A) or disagree (D).

1. Big cities are interesting and exciting places. (A / D)
2. Life is better in big cities than in rural areas. (A / D)

Vocabulary Warm-Up

Complete each sentence with the correct word or phrase. Remember to use the correct word form.

| make up | emerge | population | at the forefront |
| commercial | infrastructure | lifestyle | vicious cycle |

1. More than 30% of Peru's _____ lives in the capital, Lima.
2. As more people move away from the town, more local businesses close. It's a(n) _____.
3. Rents for _____ buildings are usually highest in city centers. That's because many companies want offices there.
4. My uncle, who lives in Osaka, has a fast and busy _____.
5. _____ projects like subway systems are expensive to build.

67

Reading Passage   Track 25

In the year 1800, cities were home to just 3% of the world's **population**. That number now exceeds 50%, and it is still rising. The largest urban centers are called "megacities," which usually refers to city centers and their surrounding areas. Megacities have attractive features as well as deep flaws. To solve them, city leaders are turning to technology.

According to the United Nations, a megacity must have a population of at least 10 million people. There were only two such places in 1950. Since then, the appeal of better jobs, schools, and **lifestyles** has drawn millions of people from the countryside. By 2016, the number of megacities had grown to 31. China was home to six of them. Not surprisingly, in 2016, two-thirds of the world's new skyscrapers were built in China.

Megacities are **commercial** powerhouses that **make up** a large part of their countries' economies. For instance, London is responsible for 22% of the UK's GDP. When cities form connections with each other in "corridors," they become even stronger. The Osaka-Nagoya-Tokyo corridor is home to around 60% of Japan's population and many world-class companies. California's Silicon Valley, stretching from San Francisco to San Jose, is home to tech giants like Google, Facebook, and Apple.

With so many people streaming into cities, new problems have **emerged**. They include increased air pollution, water shortages, and **infrastructure** shortcomings. These issues are serious in the slums of the developing world. Income inequality in India, Africa, and South America creates a **vicious cycle** that's hard to break.

Technology is **at the forefront** of efforts to extend resources to everyone. Soon, driverless electric cars may reduce air pollution and traffic congestion. When rented on an "as needed" basis, they could make it easier for people in any neighborhood to reach their jobs. Also, advances in energy production are allowing buildings to generate their own clean electricity. That reduces pollution, lessens strains on the power grid, and helps fight global warming.

Another positive tech trend is the Internet of Things. As it expands, more cars, buildings, and infrastructure systems are generating real-time data.

For example, Seoul's city government monitors GPS and other sensor data to keep traffic running smoothly. In a state-of-the-art control room, problems are met quickly and efficiently.

40　The growth of megacities is a strong trend. Their number may exceed 40 in 2030. By then, nearly five billion people are expected to live in urban areas. As these places develop, they will surely present us with new opportunities and challenges.

> **Glossary**
> feature – special point; flaw – problem; appeal – attraction; skyscraper – very tall building; powerhouse – something that's very strong; GDP – gross domestic product; corridor – hallway / lane; stream into – enter quickly or in large quantities; shortcoming – something that isn't good enough; slum – very poor district; developing world – countries that are not yet modernized or rich; strain – pressure; power grid – system supplying and monitoring electricity; state of the art – most advanced

Comprehension Check

Choose the best answer to each question.

Main Idea
1. What is the main idea?
    (A) Although megacities are quickly growing, there are enough jobs for everyone.
    (B) In 20 years, few people will live in the countryside.
    (C) Megacities are a key part of modern life, with both good and bad points.
    (D) China has more megacities than anywhere else.

Detail
2. Which of the following has drawn people to cities for decades?
    (A) The chance for a better education
    (B) The opportunity to rent electric cars
    (C) The problem of water shortages
    (D) The use of clean energy by everyone

Analysis
3. How does the Internet of Things help city governments?
    (A) By making it easier to buy products online
    (B) By supplying information very quickly
    (C) By recycling things to make cities cleaner
    (D) By designing state-of-the-art computers

Circle if each statement is true (T) or false (F).

1. Between 1950 and 2016, the number of megacities increased by 29. (T / F)

2. Only megacities which are connected via corridors are important to a country's GDP. (T / F)

● Vocabulary Check

A. Choose the best word or phrase to complete each sentence.

1. Beijing's _____ grew from 6 million in 1975 to over 20 million in 2017.
   (A) population   (B) pollution   (C) technology   (D) efficiency
2. Roads, power lines, and water systems are important parts of a city's _____.
   (A) countryside   (B) engineer   (C) vehicle   (D) infrastructure
3. As more families move to the neighborhood, rental costs keep rising. It's a(n) _____.
   (A) vicious cycle (B) world class (C) income inequality (D) water shortage
4. The area north of the Chicago River _____ the city's most popular tourist district.
   (A) grows to   (B) expects to   (C) lives in   (D) makes up
5. I love eating at a variety of restaurants, so Tokyo suits my _____.
   (A) official   (B) distance   (C) lifestyle   (D) economy

B. Choose the word or phrase that means the same as the underlined part.

1. Moscow's commercial center is home to some beautiful office buildings.
   (A) government   (B) business   (C) neighborhood (D) entertainment
2. In recent years, Lagos has emerged as one of Africa's most exciting cities.
   (A) blamed as   (B) stepped down (C) compared to   (D) come out
3. Lincoln Center is at the forefront of New York's classical music scene.
   (A) in the lead   (B) around the corner (C) before the start (D) on the road

● Grammar Building - Subject / Verb Agreement

Choose the correct word to complete each sentence.

Ex: A lot of the old neighborhoods in Paris (is / are) pretty.
Ans: A lot of the old neighborhoods in Paris *are* pretty.

1. The park that I told everyone about (is / are) over here.
2. Many skyscrapers, especially the ones 60 stories and taller, (has / have) fast elevators.
3. One of the theaters which we love (shows / show) European movies.
4. The appeal of rare books and reading tables (draw / draws) book lovers to the library.
5. India, home to five megacities, (has / have) the world's second largest population.

Grammar + Vocabulary

Put the words in the correct sentence order.

1. (years old / these commercial buildings / The majority of / are 40).

   _____

2. (our top / Repairing the / infrastructure project / before winter is / pair of bridges).

   _____

Technical Focus

A. Look at the illustration of the New Century Global Center. Then, circle if each statement is true (T) or false (F).

1. The guest services building is next to the entrance. (T / F)
2. The first aid building and the kids' slide are on opposite sides of the pool. (T / F)
3. To get to the hotel, you must first walk by the rock climbing area. (T / F)

B. Fill in the blanks with the correct word(s) from the box.

works of	people	includes
even	makes	to

China's megacities are home 1)_____ some amazing 2)_____ architecture. One of the most impressive is in Chengdu, a city of 14 million 3)_____. The New Century Global Center, which opened in 2013, is 1.7 million square meters in size. That 4)_____ it the world's largest building. It 5)_____ a giant shopping mall, movie theater, university, water park, two hotels, several office buildings, and 6)_____ an indoor beach!

Word Parts

Study the word parts in the chart. Then, read the following pairs of sentences. Circle if the second sentence is true (T) or false (F).

Word Part	Meaning	Examples
ex-	out / away	exceed, extend, excellent
-equ-	same / equal	inequality, equation, adequate
-ment	an action or its result	government, entertainment, segment

1. The machine equalizes the sounds coming out of each speaker.
   Its job is to make the speakers' sound levels the same. (T / F)

2. When Kylie dropped her ice cream, she covered her face in embarrassment.
   Dropping the ice cream made her embarrassed. (T / F)

3. There are rose bushes all around the building's exterior.
   The plants are on the outside of the building. (T / F)

4. The item can be bought in Japanese yen or the equivalent amount in US dollars.
   You have to pay an extra charge if you use US dollars. (T / F)

5. Vehicles crossing the bridge pay a fee, with the exception of emergency vehicles.
   Emergency vehicles must follow the same rules as everyone else. (T / F)

Discussion

Discuss these questions with your classmates.

1. What will megacities be like in 25 years? Name some good and bad points.
2. Think of the biggest problems in your hometown. How might technology help solve them?

13 De-Extinction

Track 26
Every day, dozens of animal, bird, and insect species go extinct. While this loss is partly due to natural causes, human activity deserves much of the blame. Scientists are working on ways to bring some species back from extinction.

Topic Warm-Up

Consider these statements. Circle if you agree (A) or disagree (D).

1. If there is a way to reverse animal extinction, we should try it. (A / D)
2. It would be interesting to see a dinosaur walking around. (A / D)

Vocabulary Warm-Up

Complete each sentence with the correct word. Remember to use the correct word form.

| ecosystem | species | survive | restore |
| extinct | underway | diversity | characteristic |

1. A rainforest is an incredible _____. Thousands of different plants and animals live there.
2. Planting trees is an excellent way to _____ a lost forest.
3. The project to clean the bay is _____. It will be completed in two years.
4. When an animal is _____, it can't be found in zoos or in the wild.
5. The most famous _____ of that type of monkey is its large nose.

Reading Passage

As **ecosystems** change over time, animal species go **extinct**. It's the natural order. However, because of human activities like hunting and logging, extinctions have accelerated to 1,000 times the normal rate. Efforts are **underway** to bring back some extinct animals. This "de-extinction" could undo some of the harm we've done while improving natural **diversity**.

Cloning is one possible recovery method for **species** which recently went extinct. The process requires an intact cell, so it would only work for animals whose cells have been preserved. The first step is to remove the cell's nucleus. A living, closely related species must also be located. The nucleus from the modern egg is replaced with that of the extinct species. The egg is then implanted into a host. In 2013, the gastric-brooding frog (which went extinct in 1983) was cloned in Australia. Though the embryos only **survived** a few days, it proved that the technique is possible.

Another method, genetic engineering, could be used for species that disappeared thousands of years ago. First, DNA samples are collected – for example, from teeth or skin. As the animal's genome is pieced together, genes for unique **characteristics** are identified. The idea is to splice those genes into the DNA of a modern relative. The woolly mammoth, extinct for 3,700 years, is a popular candidate. Modern elephants might be used as hosts. The resulting animal would be a hybrid with the general characteristics of a mammoth.

Beth Shapiro, a biologist and professor at UC Santa Cruz, has written an entire book about bringing the mammoth back. She feels there are good reasons for focusing on the wondrous animal. After mammoths went extinct, their Arctic habitat turned from grasslands into tundra. By re-introducing the species, mammoths might help **restore** the ecosystem by spreading seeds and clearing trees again. Scientists believe that species with such unique roles are good candidates for de-extinction.

However, critics note that for many species, their ecosystems and food sources are very different from the way they once were. In today's world, could extinct animals like the mammoth, passenger pigeon, or Tasmanian tiger thrive again? What's more, many ask, shouldn't we focus on keeping endangered species from going extinct? These are important and complex questions. Since DNA only lasts around one million years, one thing is certain. Long-lost species like the dinosaurs cannot be brought back. For magnificent creatures like the T-Rex, we'll have to rely on our imaginations, and the movies, to see them again.

> **Glossary**
> logging – cutting down trees; accelerate – speed up; clone – make an exact copy; intact – complete; preserve – keep and protect; nucleus – a cell's central part; embryo – animal in its developing stage (before it is born); genome – complete set of genes; unique – special; splice – insert into a DNA strand; hybrid – blend of two species; wondrous – amazing; habitat – an animal's home and surrounding area; tundra – cold, flat land with little plant or animal life; critic – person who disagrees or finds fault; thrive – be very successful; endangered – at risk of going extinct; magnificent – incredible

Comprehension Check

Choose the best answer to each question.

Main Idea
1. What is the main idea?
    (A) Even if de-extinction works, hunting and logging will continue.
    (B) Every species of animal plays an important role in its ecosystem.
    (C) Genetic engineering might create new environmental problems.
    (D) De-extinction could restore part of our lost natural diversity.

Detail
2. How might the woolly mammoth help its original habitat?
    (A) By moving seeds from place to place
    (B) By allowing the gastric-brooding frog to thrive again
    (C) By making the tundra even larger
    (D) By giving elephants a safe, new ecosystem to live in

Analysis
3. What does the article suggest about de-extinction?
    (A) Any animal can be brought back, no matter when it went extinct.
    (B) We only need a few strands of DNA to clone an animal.
    (C) For genetic engineering, DNA can be taken from different body parts.
    (D) Cloning small animals is easier than cloning large ones.

Circle if each statement is true (T) or false (F).

1. The host species for a cloned animal must be related to the extinct species. (T / F)
2. The technique shown in movies for bringing back dinosaurs is now possible. (T / F)

Vocabulary Check

A. Choose the best word to complete each sentence.

1. The African bush elephant is the largest animal _____ on land.
   (A) technique (B) critic (C) habitat (D) species
2. People love visiting Hawaii for its _____ of plants and flowers.
   (A) candidate (B) diversity (C) creature (D) professor
3. The science writer's best _____ is her attention to detail.
   (A) estimate (B) characteristic (C) researcher (D) imagination
4. In dry _____ like deserts, finding enough water is a daily struggle.
   (A) ecosystems (B) methods (C) hybrids (D) relatives
5. Large, protected parks keep endangered animals from going _____.
   (A) wondrous (B) intact (C) extinct (D) preserved

B. Choose the word that means the same as the underlined part.

1. It's hard to <u>survive</u> in extremely cold or hot places, but some people are able to do so.
   (A) live (B) cook (C) work (D) walk
2. Please send me a message once the experiment is <u>underway</u>.
   (A) happening (B) finished (C) cancelled (D) changing
3. Do you think it will be possible to <u>restore</u> the wetlands?
   (A) rename (B) remove (C) repair (D) resist

Grammar Building - Present Perfect

Choose the correct word to complete each sentence.

Ex: The botany professor (has / have) written several interesting articles.
Ans: The botany professor *has* written several interesting articles.

1. Due to hunting, some big cat species (has / have) gone extinct.
2. (Has / Have) the full genome of the snow monkey been sequenced?
3. No, the full contents of the report (has / have) not been published yet.
4. One of my friends (has / have) studied the social habits of giraffes.
5. Kenya (has / have) become famous for its rich diversity of wildlife.

Grammar + Vocabulary

Put the words in the correct sentence order.

1. (has been / in detail / The great white shark's / studied / ecosystem).
   _____

2. (the winter / have / the bees / survived / Most of).
   _____

Technical Focus

A. Look at the illustration of a CRISPR-Cas9 system. Then, circle if each statement is true (T) or false (F).

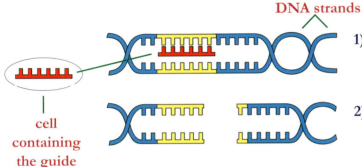

1. The guide RNA and Cas9 protein are in separate cells. (T / F)
2. The Cas9 protein cuts two strands of DNA. (T / F)
3. Before the DNA is cut, the cell tries to repair itself. (T / F)

B. Fill in the blanks with the correct word(s) from the box.

as well as	in	can be
one of	the	field

The 1)_____ of genetic engineering may help extinct and living animals, 2)_____ people. 3)_____ the main tools for gene editing is called CRISPR-Cas9. The first step is making a strand of RNA 4)_____ a lab. Next, using a CRISPR-Cas9 system, 5)_____ RNA is used to locate a specific DNA sequence. Once located, the DNA sequence is cut by a protein such as Cas9. Then, a strand of DNA 6)_____ removed, replaced, or altered.

77

Word Parts

Study the word parts in the chart. Then, read the following pairs of sentences. Circle if the second sentence is true (T) or false (F).

Word Part	Meaning	Examples
col-	with / together	collect, college, collide
-spec-	look / see	species, inspect, speculate
-ic	related to / having a quality	genetic, characteristic, arctic

1. Thousands of spectators lined up for the panda bear exhibit.
   Many people waited to see the bears. (T / F)

2. Mr. Yoshida is one of Mayumi's colleagues.
   Mayumi works with Mr. Yoshida. (T / F)

3. The microscopic creature lives at the bottom of the ocean.
   The life form can easily be seen without using a microscope. (T / F)

4. Paul and Sheila have different perspectives on de-extinction.
   They see the topic in the same way. (T / F)

5. The robotic equipment can carry out experiments without getting tired.
   The experiments are done by robots. (T / F)

Discussion

Discuss these questions with your classmates.

1. If you could bring back any extinct animal, which one would you choose? Why?

2. Do you agree that we should focus on protecting endangered species? Or should de-extinction projects get more attention? Explain your answer.

14 Muon Imaging: Using Physics to See the Unseen

Track 28

Tools like X-ray machines work well for seeing inside small objects. However, scanning large objects is much more difficult. Thanks to discoveries in physics, we can now look inside almost anything, including mountains. It all starts with particles from deep space.

Topic Warm-Up

Consider these statements. Circle if you agree (A) or disagree (D).

1. Scientific research benefits governments as well as businesses. (A / D)
2. Experts in different fields should work together whenever possible. (A / D)

Vocabulary Warm-Up

Complete each sentence with the correct word or phrase. Remember to use the correct word form.

| theory | preserve | structure | dense |
| breakthrough | internal | line up | impact |

1. Dozens of archaeologists are _____ to participate in the African study.
2. What's your _____ about the power loss? I think it might have to do with the weather.
3. The material is thin but _____. It blocks most sounds from passing through.
4. Our team just made a(n) _____. We discovered a way to double the instrument's range.
5. The 3000-year-old object was placed in a special case to _____ it.

79

Reading Passage Track 29

Cosmic rays, which travel great distances through space, are a threat to astronauts. However, when they reach the Earth's atmosphere, most of them break up and become harmless. The breakup leads to the creation of subatomic particles called muons. Physicists have learned to map their movements, with exciting applications in geology, mining, and other fields.

After muons form, they move towards the Earth's surface at nearly the speed of light. They can penetrate **dense** matter, including water, rocks, and even mountains. Such objects slow muons down, change their direction, or stop them completely. Researchers use special plates, or "detectors," to collect the muons which pass through an object. After analyzing the data, a density map of the object is made. The result is an image similar to an X-ray.

For early uses of muon imaging, it was only possible to create 2D images. For example, in 1954 Professor Eric George set up detectors to measure the ice and rock above the Guthega-Munyang tunnel in Australia. The following decade, Nobel Prize winner Luis Alvarez studied the way muons passed through the Pyramid of Khafre in Egypt. Archaeology is an excellent use of the technology, since it is harmless to ancient **structures**.

An important **breakthrough** was made in 2002 at Los Alamos National Laboratory. Researchers learned to chart the way a muon's path changes after **impacting** matter. With detectors placed on both sides of an object, an **internal** 3D map of the object can be created. Such "muon tomography" was used to map the inside of the damaged Fukushima reactors in 2015. The collected data may help with the cleanup effort. Another imaging system in the Bahamas scans cargo to look for contraband.

Recently, archaeologists have **lined up** to use advances in the field. In 2015, an international team from Japan, Canada, Egypt, and France began using muon imaging to study pyramids in Egypt. They discovered a large, previously unknown structure inside the Great Pyramid. It was the first discovery of its kind in over 100 years! Another imaging team in Mexico studied the Pyramid of the Sun and found structural weaknesses.

Such efforts teach us about historical treasures while helping us **preserve** them.

40 Muon imaging has other important uses. We can look inside volcanoes for clues about when they may erupt. Liquid CO_2, buried underground so it doesn't add to global warming, might also be monitored this way. The technology is the perfect meeting of scientific **theory** and real-world practice. It will be fascinating to see how it is used in the coming years.

> **Glossary**
> cosmic rays – fast-moving particles in space; threat – danger; atmosphere – the gases surrounding the Earth; harmless – safe; subatomic – smaller than an atom; penetrate – go through; detector – device that determines if something is present; pyramid – ancient stone structure with sides shaped like a triangle; archaeology – the study of history and past cultures through examining objects; tomography – making an image of the inside of an object or area; cargo – shipped item; contraband – illegal item; clue – hint / piece of information; erupt – explode

Comprehension Check

Choose the best answer to each question.

Main Idea
1. What is the main idea?
    (A) Producing a 2D muon scan is similar to taking an X-ray.
    (B) By showing us what's inside objects, muon imaging has practical uses.
    (C) Archaeologists from different countries enjoy working together.
    (D) Because of their size, mountains are difficult to study using muons.

Detail
2. When did Luis Alvarez use muon imaging to study a pyramid?
    (A) In the 1940s   (B) In the 1950s   (C) In the 1960s   (D) In the 2000s

Analysis
3. Why is muon imaging so useful in archaeology?
    (A) It makes it easier to remove objects from pyramids.
    (B) It has been providing good 3D images since the 1950s.
    (C) It tells us exactly when ancient structures were built.
    (D) It doesn't harm the buildings that are being studied.

Circle if each statement is true (T) or false (F).

1. Muons form in space before cosmic rays reach the Earth's atmosphere. (T / F)
2. Muon imaging may tell us more about volcanic activity. (T / F)

Vocabulary Check

A. Choose the best word or phrase to complete each sentence.

1. After the earthquake, volunteers from all around _____ to help.
   (A) broke up   (B) looked for   (C) led to   (D) lined up
2. Museums both _____ and display items that were used in space missions.
   (A) damage   (B) erupt   (C) become   (D) preserve
3. The _____ of Albert Einstein have solved some scientific mysteries. One of them explains why muons are able to travel so far.
   (A) objects   (B) theories   (C) decades   (D) movements
4. The rock is so _____. How are we going to cut through it with these tools?
   (A) dense   (B) near   (C) slow   (D) real
5. The Hubble Telescope has led to important _____ in astronomy. It has shown us some amazing sights for the first time.
   (A) atmospheres   (B) tunnels   (C) breakthroughs   (D) volcanoes

B. Choose the word that means the same as the underlined part.

1. Does the device have an internal power source?
   (A) inside   (B) incomplete   (C) inactive   (D) incorrect
2. The moon's surface has been impacted by many asteroids.
   (A) built   (B) mapped   (C) hit   (D) seen
3. The structure which holds the telescope needs a roof that opens and closes.
   (A) science   (B) location   (C) blueprint   (D) building

Grammar Building - Comparatives + Superlatives

Choose the correct word to complete each sentence.

Ex: The Large Hadron Collider is the world's (bigger / biggest) particle accelerator.
Ans: The Large Hadron Collider is the world's *biggest* particle accelerator.

1. The tunnel is (wider / more wide) here than in other spots.
2. The Great Pyramid is the (larger / largest) pyramid in Giza, Egypt. No others are as big.
3. Our equipment is (as advanced / less advanced) than the equipment at Los Alamos.
4. For some tomography projects, muons are (more useful / most useful) than X-rays.
5. Italy has some of the (oldest / most old) buildings in Europe.

Grammar + Vocabulary

Put the words in the correct sentence order.

1. (genetics lab's / It's / impressive breakthrough / most / the).
   _____

2. (than the / less clear / These / previous ones / internal scans are).
   _____

Technical Focus

A. Look at the illustration of a muon imaging cargo scanner. Then, circle if each statement is true (T) or false (F).

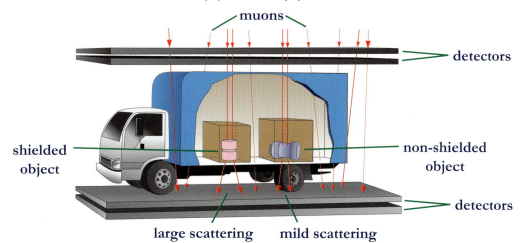

1. Muons are detected when they enter and leave an area. (T / F)
2. Impacting certain objects changes a muon's direction. (T / F)
3. If an object is shielded, muons will not impact it. (T / F)

B. Fill in the blanks with the correct word(s) from the box.

| researchers | set up | less than |
| creating | takes | greatly |

Traditional 2D muon imaging 1)_____ time. Once the detector plates are positioned, 2)_____ wait for the muons to arrive. Gathering enough muons and 3)_____ an image can take weeks. With 3D muon tomography, the process is 4)_____ sped up. In the Bahamas, Decision Sciences 5)_____ a system based on the Los Alamos advances. The system scans a cargo container in 6)_____ a minute.

Word Parts

Study the word parts in the chart. Then, read the following pairs of sentences. Circle if the second sentence is true (T) or false (F).

Word Part	Meaning	Examples
pre-	before	previously, predict, preschool
-graph-	write / draw	tomography, graphics, holograph
-ness	being in a condition	weakness, happiness, kindness

1. This Andy Warhol lithograph was made in 1972.
   It's a movie about Andy Warhol's life. (T / F)

2. If more batteries are used, it will prevent future power supply problems.
   The suggestion is to reduce the number of batteries to avoid power problems. (T / F)

3. The darkness of the room made it difficult to read.
   It wasn't bright enough to read comfortably. (T / F)

4. Luis Alvarez's work on pyramids predates the 2015 project.
   The scholars all studied the pyramids at the same time. (T / F)

5. Travis was excited to receive his favorite singer's autograph.
   The singer signed his name for Travis. (T / F)

Discussion

Discuss these questions with your classmates.

1. If you could choose something to scan with a muon detector, what would it be? What is your reason for that choice?

2. Particle physics and other research fields can be very expensive. Sometimes it takes years to see any benefits. What's your opinion about spending a lot on "pure science"? Should countries spend more or less than they are spending now?

15 Our Clean Future

Track 30

Many efforts are underway to heal the environment, restore the oceans, and fight climate change. This hard work is yielding results. Improvements in energy, transportation, and other areas are providing hope for a bright, clean future.

● Topic Warm-Up

Consider these statements. Circle if you agree (A) or disagree (D).

1. No matter how old you are, you can make the world a better place. (A / D)

2. In general, I feel positive about the future. (A / D)

● Vocabulary Warm-Up

Complete each sentence with the correct word or phrase. Remember to use the correct word form.

| altogether | practical | resource | make a difference |
| invest | phase out | affordable | renewable energy |

1. To meet its energy needs, the computer maker will _____ 100 million yen in solar equipment.
2. This mobile app is really _____. It shows you the distance you've walked and the number of calories you've burned.
3. Three staff members from each branch attended the meeting. _____, 18 people were there.
4. Wind power is a common source of _____.
5. We are _____ this type of packaging. By next year, our boxes will be 30% smaller.

Reading Passage Track 31

We live in a time of serious challenges, along with real hope for solving them. Climate change, dirty air, and polluted oceans are unfortunate products of 100 years of modern development. At the same time, there is growing interest in the environment among citizens, businesses, and governments. If we use our **resources** and technology wisely, we can build a clean, prosperous future together.

Renewable energy will help us combat pollution and climate change. Sources like wind and solar power are becoming **affordable** and widely used. In 2016, $287 billion was **invested** in clean energy projects. Developing countries like India, China, and Brazil are among the leaders in the field. For example, India recently built the world's largest solar plant in just eight months. In the developed world, California is setting an excellent example. The state's near-term target is to receive 50% of its energy from renewable sources.

Automobiles make our lives convenient, but they are heavy polluters. Thanks to electric vehicles (EVs), cars are getting a clean, new image. There were just 1,000 EVs on the road in 2005. By 2016, the number had jumped to two million. With companies like Nissan and Tesla leading the way, EVs are becoming **practical**, affordable, and even fashionable. That's great news, since during their lifetimes, EVs create half the greenhouse gas emissions of conventional cars. France and the UK are two of the countries planning to **phase out** conventional cars **altogether**.

One precious resource that needs attention is our oceans. They are full of plastic waste. In the Pacific Ocean, the so-called "Great Pacific Garbage Patch" contains an estimated five trillion pieces of plastic. A possible solution was put forward by the Dutch inventor Boyan Slat. When he was a teenager, he founded The Ocean Cleanup. The organization hopes to clear 50% of the Garbage Patch within 10 years. Other groups are focusing on cleaning beaches. Trash Hero, a group formed in Thailand, has chapters in several countries. They have already picked up 200,000 kilograms of garbage just in Thailand.

35 Many other efforts for a greener future are in motion. Biofuels and hydropower are among the clean energy sources receiving attention. Battery makers are making incredible advances, which is great news for EVs. And screens are being placed in rivers to block plastics from flowing into oceans. Just by using our own cloth bags at shops instead
40 of taking plastic bags, you and I can **make a difference**, too. Through a focused effort, we can make our world cleaner, safer, and more beautiful.

> **Glossary**
> prosperous – successful / wealthy; combat – fight; solar plant – place that collects sunlight and turns it into electricity; near-term – happening soon;
> conventional car – car with a gas or diesel engine; precious – important / valuable;
> patch – area; chapter – branch / unit; biofuel – fuel from an organic source such as corn;
> hydropower – electricity generated by flowing water

Comprehension Check

Choose the best answer to each question.

Main Idea
1. What is the main idea?
   (A) Almost $300 billion was invested in clean energy in 2016.
   (B) Most people want to make a positive difference during their lives.
   (C) Many things are happening to make the world a cleaner place.
   (D) It will take years to remove all the plastic waste from the oceans.

Detail
2. Which place has a goal of getting one-half of its energy from clean sources?
   (A) California   (B) China   (C) Thailand   (D) India

Analysis
3. What does the article suggest about developing countries?
   (A) They believe rich countries should spend more on clean energy.
   (B) They invest more on wind power than on hydropower or solar power.
   (C) They build new solar plants once every eight months, on average.
   (D) They are working hard to get more energy from renewable sources.

Circle if each statement is true (T) or false (F).

1. Conventional cars produce twice the greenhouse gas emissions of EVs. (T / F)
2. Trash Hero's chapters are all in Thailand. (T / F)

● Vocabulary Check

A. Choose the best word or phrase to complete each sentence.
1. We ride our bikes to reduce air pollution. It isn't much, but it _____ .
   (A) makes a difference   (B) flows into oceans
   (C) gets a new image   (D) creates more emissions
2. Water cools the factory pipes. That makes it an important _____ for us.
   (A) environment   (B) resource   (C) symbol   (D) chapter
3. Ordering supplies online is more _____ than buying them in stores.
   (A) affordable   (B) prosperous   (C) estimated   (D) beautiful
4. My dad wants to _____ money in the shop. It sells organic fruits and vegetables.
   (A) solve   (B) build   (C) invest   (D) combat
5. In a country with large, open spaces, wind power would be a perfect type of _____ .
   (A) climate change   (B) renewable energy
   (C) solar plant   (D) electric vehicle

B. Choose the word or phrase that means the same as the underlined part.
1. Both in cities and on highways, electric cars are practical vehicles.
   (A) fast   (B) popular   (C) small   (D) useful
2. Altogether, 52 students helped clean the campus over the weekend.
   (A) In total   (B) Either way   (C) Besides that   (D) On time
3. The city will phase out conventional buses by 2035.
   (A) stop using   (B) keep charging   (C) begin fixing   (D) try cleaning

● Grammar Building - Word Forms

Choose the correct word to complete each sentence.

Ex: The lake is (pollute / polluted / pollution), so we don't swim in it.
Ans: The lake is *polluted*, so we don't swim in it.

1. The (electric / electricity / electrical) for my cousin's home comes from solar panels.
2. Can you (afford / affordable / afforded) such a nice jacket?
3. We're waiting for them to (estimate / estimating / estimated) the size of the oil spill.
4. I thought the drawing was (beauty / beautiful / beautifully) done.
5. Used bottles, paper, and other (waste / wasteful / wasted) should be recycled.

Grammar + Vocabulary

Put the words in the correct sentence order.

1. (more affordable / Solar power / 20 years ago / is much / than).

   _____

2. (paper memos / Our / phasing out / is / office).

   _____

Technical Focus

A. Look at the illustration of a solar-powered home. Then, circle if each statement is true (T) or false (F).

1) Solar panels (turn sunlight into DC electric current)

4) Meter (monitors the flow of excess electricity to the grid)

2) Inverter (converts electricity from DC to AC power)

3) Electric panel (manages the use of electricity by the home)

1. Sunlight strikes the top of the solar panels to start the electricity generation process. (T / F)
2. Before the electricity is used in a home, it passes through an inverter. (T / F)
3. The electricity added to the grid is in the form of DC power. (T / F)

B. Fill in the blanks with the correct word from the box.

| current | by | finally |
| the | electrical | called |

Sunlight travels in the form of particles 1)_____ photons. When photons are absorbed 2)_____ a solar panel, they generate an electric current. That 3)_____ then passes through a device called an inverter. It changes 4)_____ electricity from DC to AC power. 5)_____, the electricity is usable for a home or office. Surplus energy can be sent through a meter and added to the 6)_____ grid.

89

Word Parts

Study the word parts in the chart. Then, read the following pairs of sentences. Circle if the second sentence is true (T) or false (F).

Word Part	Meaning	Examples
kilo-	one thousand	kilogram, kilobyte, kilometer
-hydr(o)-	water	hydropower, dehydrated, hydrogen
-ous	having such a quality	prosperous, joyous, marvelous

1. The hikers made sure to stay hydrated during their day out.
   They drank enough water during their hike. (T / F)

2. There is one kiloton of metal in the scrapyard.
   The scrapyard has exactly 100 tons of metal. (T / F)

3. My brother lives in a mountainous area.
   There are mountains around his home. (T / F)

4. The street has several fire hydrants that are available for use.
   Firefighters have more than one water source, if needed. (T / F)

5. Overnight, a mysterious green spot formed in the center of the fountain.
   The reason for the appearance of the spot is known. (T / F)

Discussion

Discuss these questions with your classmates.

1. Besides the oceans, what other areas need to be cleaned up? What is the best way to clean them?

2. If you could spend one day a week helping an environmental cause, what would it be? (ex: planting trees, volunteering at a park, etc.)

著作権法上，無断複写・複製は禁じられています。

Science and Tech Sense [B-884]

1 刷	2019 年 4 月 1 日
5 刷	2023 年 3 月 7 日

著　者　アンドルー E. ベネット　　　Andrew E. Bennett

発行者　南雲一範　Kazunori Nagumo
発行所　株式会社　南雲堂
　　　　〒 162-0801　東京都新宿区山吹町 361
　　　　NAN'UN-DO Co., Ltd.
　　　　361 Yamabuki-cho, Shinjuku-ku, Tokyo 162-0801, Japan
　　　　振替口座：00160-0-46863
　　　　TEL: 03-3268-2311（営業部：学校関係）
　　　　　　　03-3268-2384（営業部：書店関係）
　　　　　　　03-3268-2387（編集部）
　　　　FAX: 03-3269-2486
編集者　加藤　敦

Technical Focus illustrations	Irene Fu
装　丁	銀月堂
組　版	Office haru
検　印	省　略
コード	ISBN978-4-523-17884-2　C0082

Printed in Japan

E-mail　nanundo@post.email.ne.jp
URL　https://www.nanun-do.co.jp/